Preaching To A TV Generation

The Sermon In The Electronic Age

Michael Rogness

CSS Publishing Company, Inc.
Lima, Ohio

PREACHING TO A TV GENERATION

Copyright © 1994 by
The CSS Publishing Company, Inc.
Lima, Ohio

Library of Congress Cataloging-in-Publication Data

Rogness, Michael.
    Preaching to a TV generation : preaching for an electronic age / by Michael Rogness.
        p.   cm.
    ISBN 1-55673-838-2
    1. Preaching. 2. Television broadcasting—Religious aspects—Christianity. I. Title.
BV4211.2.R64   1994
251—dc20   93-47208
                                                                            CIP

ISBN 1-55673-838-2   PRINTED IN U.S.A.

To Eva
in admiration
for the ministry of the Word
which she does so faithfully

Table Of Contents

Preface

Harry Emerson Fosdick was an advocate and practitioner of problem/solution preaching. Such sermons address and seek to solve specific problems of living. This is a problem/solution book. It confronts and seeks to help solve a specific problem of contemporary preaching. The problem facing every preacher today is a television-saturated congregation so acclimated to glitz and snappy sound bites that it is difficult to capture and retain their attention long enough to create a vital encounter with the life-transforming message of the gospel.

The first two chapters describe and analyze "the TV revolution" and "the TV audience." The rest of the book presents an array of specific recommendations and concrete illustrations to help the preacher communicate meaningfully with television-soaked people. This is not an abstract treatise on homiletical theory. It is a clear practical guide abounding in insightful suggestions for preachers who wish to be heard and heeded by their congregations. If you want to be a better preacher, ponder these pages and seek to practice what they teach. You will be a better preacher for doing so.

I strongly affirm Rogness' wisdom when he says, "The age of reading before an audience is gone!" and "Reading a sermon is the best way to kill it." I wonder, however, if his solution to sermons that are read, and therefore dead, is sufficiently radical? He believes that "for long-term growth and improvement in preaching there is no substitute for careful preparation of a manuscript" and offers specific suggestions on how to preach from a manuscript without reading it. I believe that careful ordering of thought and extensive writing of vital points are absolutely essential but that when preparing to speak, and not to read, there is no need to prepare a formal manuscript and that to do so is often more hurtful than helpful. My personal preference is to prepare a detailed sermon outline that lets me see the plan of development and in which much, but not all, is written out in full. With such a plan in the pulpit I can't read it but am enabled to rethink my thought at the moment of utterance and this, I believe, is an essential characteristic of vital, direct communication.

With that single exception I commend this book without reservation. There is great stuff here! It clearly confronts a central problem facing preachers in the television age and with winsome wisdom helps us all to be the better preachers we want, and are called to be. Study it from beginning to end and when near the end, take time to ponder what is said about "preaching and pastoral ministry." That is a subject worthy of another book and on the basis of his brief comments here, I hope Rogness will write it.

Lowell O. Erdahl, Bishop
St. Paul Area Synod
Evangelical Lutheran Church in America

Foreword

Buried in the 95 Theses, which Martin Luther tacked to the south door of the Wittenberg Castle Church in 1517, was the time bomb which ultimately detonated the explosion of the Reformation. Thesis 62 states: "The true treasure of the church is the most holy gospel of the glory and grace of God."[1] The very heart of the Reformation was the proclamation of this "most holy gospel of the glory and grace of God." The Word of God was spoken, taught, sung, studied and meditated upon as never before in the history of the church.

This "most holy gospel" is still the precious treasure of the church, and the preaching of God's Word is still the primary calling of a pastor. That will never change. One of the standard Bible verses read at the ordination of a new pastor is Paul's plea for preaching: "And how are they to believe in him of whom they have never heard? And how are they to hear without a preacher?" (Romans 10:14) That wonderful good news of the gospel swept through the first century with astonishing power.

Today, however, people often seem bored with it all. Where has the power gone?

The crisis of preaching is that we face an audience accustomed to new forms of communication. The way people listen is shaped by today's most dominant medium — television. We live in a communication world vastly different from that of our grandparents, and yet we preach about the same as preachers did before the arrival of television.

It isn't working very well.

Someone has said, "The age of preaching is dead." That's not true and never will be. The gospel has always been conveyed

9

primarily by speaking it to people. But people listen and hear differently in this world of television. When we preachers understand the dynamics of this new world, then the gospel can ring with new vigor and life in our preaching.

The first two chapters set the stage by looking at this new world of communication. Chapter one describes the sweeping changes brought by television. Chapter two analyzes the television audience, listing the ways electronic communication has changed the way we listen. The following five chapters suggest what preachers can do in the face of these changes — in terms of language, structure, creativity and delivery.

Michael Rogness

Chapter 1

The TV Revolution

As the dominant medium of social expression, television is pervasive in a profound way that we seldom recognize fully. Because most of us get most of our information about the society most of the time from television, it becomes the primary social fact of our lives.[2]

— James Monaco

Preaching Today

While visiting many congregations I am constantly astonished to hear how much complaining there is about preaching. Faithful churchgoers find themselves wondering, "What's happened to good preaching?" "Where have all the good preachers gone?"

Preaching has fallen on hard times.

There are several reasons for this malaise. Some pastors don't work very hard on their sermons. Some are out of touch with their congregations. Others are ineffective public speakers. Much preaching is theological fluff. Another part of the problem is that people in the pews have such a wide range of expectations from the sermon that it is impossible to satisfy everybody.

Yet the truth is that many pastors work hard at their preaching, but sense it is not effective, and they cannot put their finger on the reasons why.

A fundamental reason for this situation is that we live in the midst of a massive communications revolution, which we have only begun to understand. This revolution inevitably affects the way people listen to sermons, and if we fail to take this into account in preaching we will not reach our audience.

The Communications Upheaval

John Killinger, professor of preaching at Vanderbilt Divinity School in Nashville, Tennessee, set out to identify "some of the primary characteristics of our cultural epoch which ... might make important differences in the way we worship." His primary observation was:

> *"For one thing, the world has become Mediaville." We live with television, stereo, videotape, recording machines, computers, cameras, projectors, synthesizers, printing machines, duplicating machines — every imaginable mechanical extension of the self. More than anything ... they have changed the time in which we live.*[3]

We live in a radically new age of communication, which has a deep and permanent impact on how people listen. Richard A. Jensen, long-time preacher on the "Lutheran Vespers" national radio program, calls it the "post-literate age," in which electronic communication has replaced a reading culture and requires a radical shift in how we preach.[4] Failure to realize this huge change dooms us to ineffective preaching.

The predominant feature of this revolution is television, which in the last 40 years has become the primary medium of public communication. It is a vastly different medium of communication from reading, and it is even quite different from person-to-person speaking.

We are preaching to a different audience than what existed a few decades ago. I call it the "TV audience," people whose primary medium of information and entertainment is television. This audience receives information and processes what they've seen and heard far differently than their grandparents.[5] If we preach to them the same way we preached to previous generations, we shall fail to communicate. If we preachers do not understand the TV audience, we will be as effective as a movie theater which tries to draw crowds with jerky old black-and-white silent movies in this age of wide-screen, brilliant colors, Dolby sound and computer-produced graphics.

The concern of this book is: How has television affected the way people listen to and apprehend the spoken word, and how should we preachers respond?

From Orality To Print

Ancient societies were oral. Without alphabets the only means of communicating words was to speak person to person. History and culture were transmitted by storytellers and poets speaking to their listeners.

In oral societies language was highly poetic, because rhythm and rhyme enabled people to remember. Stories were rich with figures of speech, color and repetition. Speaking often took on a ritual aura, with villagers gathered ceremoniously around the speaker. In the schools of the ancient world the art of speaking and persuasion — rhetoric — was at the heart of the academic curriculum.

The printing of the Gutenberg Bible on movable type over 500 years ago launched the age of mass-produced printing, and the shift from oral communication to printed communication was enormously accelerated. No longer were books limited to monasteries, churches and wealthy homes. Families could have the wisdom and learning of centuries at their fingertips on living room shelves. Communication through reading changed the oral world to a predominantly print world.

The printed page changed the style of communication drastically from that of the oral storyteller. The language of poetry and color gave way to prose and logic, because the printed page was suited to detailed, sequential, logical development of thought. Figures of speech designed to aid memory gave way to economical, precise prose, where one did not have to repeat words or ideas already stated.

The work and influence of great scholars spread across Europe. The work of Augustine, Aquinas, Newton, Kant and other such thinkers would have been inconceivable in an oral culture. Massive amounts of information could be packed into a small space. The sheer amount of information exploded, because one could keep track of it on paper and didn't have

13

to remember it all. Modern science was born, because scholars could build upon the massive amount of information readily available on book shelves. They could write down their own discoveries on paper for thousands to read.

We became accustomed to learning through our eyes rather than through our ears. What student hasn't asked, "Why should I go hear the lecture, when I can sit here and read books a lot easier and faster?"

Naturally the world of print shaped preaching. Sermons were carefully prepared manuscripts, presenting a logical line of thinking. An idea could be expanded upon and considered from different view points. Preachers worked diligently on their manuscripts and read them from the pulpit. People became accustomed to lengthy expository sermons.

And Now Television, The Electronic Medium

Oral and print cultures were both verbal. For centuries, whether spoken or written, *words* were the primary medium of communication in the western world. But today's new technology has vastly expanded the possibilities of communication. Roy P. Madsen, who teaches film production, notes that:

> *film and television, . . . now offer forms of communication emancipated from the culture bound concepts of the printed word or immobile art. Visual meanings, expressed in movement, may now be sent from mind to mind through the eyes.*[6]

This has vastly expanded the possibilities of communication. From the old oral stage of communication, followed by the print stage, we have now entered the electronic age of communication.

The shift from orality to print took centuries, but television has bullied its way past all other forms of communication in a very short time. It has become the predominant means not only of information but also of entertainment for almost everyone in the western world. It has caused a massive change in how we listen, learn and, yes, even think.

People today receive information about the world around them primarily not by speaking to each other, not even by reading a printed page, but by seeing images and listening to words transmitted electronically on a screen. Unlike a stage drama, where real people appear in front of us, the images of television and film are electronically conveyed. The television image darts about the world, or blitzes me with 50 images in one 30-second advertisement.

It is a more profound change than previous verbal stages of communication. Television combines seeing and hearing, but with a whole new set of dynamics which make it different from speaking or reading.

A Visual Medium

Radio is a medium of hearing, with no visual component at all. Print is a medium of seeing letters on the page, with no hearing. At first glance television appears to be a return to the oral stage of communication, because we both see and hear people speak. It is, however, profoundly different, a new medium with its own distinctive dynamic.

Television is primarily a visual medium. The picture and the graphics are the heart of communication, not the words spoken. We speak of talk shows on television, but after watching them British writer Peter Conrad concluded:

> On television, conversation has become a spectator sport ... Television talk is not conversation but a celebration of visibility ... Talk on television isn't meant to be listened to. The words merely gain for us the time to look at the talker.[1]

Television does not lend itself to speaking more than a minute or two. Viewers quickly tire of the sight of one speaker from one angle. Television preachers have learned that to maintain viewer interest as they preach, several cameras with different angles are used, zooming in and out, and occasionally showing the audience, the stained glass, fountains, flowers, or whatever — in order to keep the image moving as

15

they speak. Politicians use 30-second spots, knowing that few people would sit through a lengthy speech on television. Presidential debates are broken up into tiny segments of back-and-forth conversation, despite the foolishness of presenting a national economic policy in three minutes!

The visual nature of television has influenced other media as well. Magazines and newspapers carry many more pictures than they did in the past. Compare a newspaper or magazine from 50 years ago to those of today. They include many more pictures today than in the past. Teachers in schools, pastors in churches, leaders in business, campaigners in politics — everybody pays more attention to such things as image, logos and interest-catching devices to keep their audiences.

Infotainment

It is easy for preachers to become cynical about the realities of television. As a medium it is best suited for entertainment, and the television audience tends to expect sports, education and information to be presented in an entertaining way.[8] No doubt that same conditioning shapes their expectations of worship services. There is also a premium on glamour, and plain people have little chance of becoming television stars. Would Abraham Lincoln or Charles Taft have a chance in today's presidential election?

Information, education and entertainment are all rolled into one medium on screen. Was Oliver Stone's 1991 film *JFK* a presentation of history, a documentary, an argument for one view, an art form, or entertainment? For the most people in the audience it was all of the above, because films blur the distinctions. Books are suited to careful analysis and historical examination, but screen images are not. Columnist Ellen Goodman described the controversy about *JFK* as "a fuss made by a generation that reads and writes for the minds of a generation that watches and rewinds." Her concern was not the actual historical argument about the assassination, but the way electronic communication has changed all the rules of public rhetoric. She coins a new word to describe the new reality: "infotainment."

Those of us who are print people — writers and readers — are losing ground to the visual people — producers and viewers. The younger generation gets its information and infotainment from television and movies. Less information. More infotainment. The franchise over reality is passing hands.[9]

It's no wonder we have become television junkies. The statistics of television watching are staggering. The average American today spends vastly more time in front of the television screen than in conversation with others, or reading newspapers, books or magazines. The average adult in America watches television four to five hours a day, more on weekends. We spend more total hours in front of television than on the job. In a lifetime the average American spends the equivalent of 13 years and four months watching television, far more time than in working, conversing with friends and family, physical activity, education, or reading. The only activity that outranks time spent in front of the tube is sleeping!

The statistics among young people are even higher. By the age of 18 the average youth has spent more time watching television than attending school. Among children, watching television far outranks playing or conversing with other people.

Some days our conversation shrinks to daily business items and idle small talk. If you are living with a family, figure out how much time you conversed with a spouse or a child yesterday and compare it with how much time you watched television. I know only one family and one individual who live without a television set!

A Wholistic Medium

Electronic communication is more wholistic than speech or print alone, because it bombards our whole person. Not

17

only are both eyes and ears captured, but the passage pene-
trates deep into our subconscious in ways we are not even aware
of. It engages not only the left (verbal, linear, reasoning) side
of our brain, but also the right side as well (spacial, impres-
sionable, feeling).

Television and film overwhelm our senses with an emotional
impact more immediate and powerful than speech or print
alone. The public opposition to the war in Vietnam was un-
doubtedly accelerated when people saw the gruesome nature
of war in their living rooms every night. We get a feel for po-
litical candidates by seeing them close-up on the screen. The
destruction of the rainforests becomes more graphic when we
watch the giant trees thunder to the ground. We can see and
hear Luciano Pavarotti or the King's College choirboys from
our living room chairs.

Because electronic communication engages the whole person, we have learned how integral non-verbal factors are in
communication. This is a harsh reality, especially to a politi-
cal candidate who may be homely and dull from the podium,
but it is a reality. It also means that if a pastor speaks in a
stern and angry fashion, no one in the audience will hear the
message of God's love. Communication is more complex than
we have previously thought, but understanding the wholistic
nature of communication and the importance of non-verbal
factors can help us a great deal in preaching.

An Impersonal Medium

The nature of television carries with it a huge irony: It is
an immensely powerful medium, saturating us with constant
entertainment. Yet as an electronic medium it is wholly impersonal. Very seldom do I see anybody on television I know
personally, and the people on the screen are a long way away
from me. Even if my closest friend would appear on television in my living room, I am only a spectator and can't talk
to him. I can peel potatoes, read a magazine or even talk to

somebody else without offending the person on the screen. I can turn them off without irritating them. I don't have to listen at all. Many people keep the television on just to have company in the house, paying hardly any attention to it. Furthermore, frequent commercial breaks condition us to shift our attention frequently from what we're watching.

Television is the predominant means of communication in our age, using our whole sensory range as no other medium, and yet because we can turn it on and off at will, we are trained to become passive listeners! Instead of producing better listeners, television has produced an audience which doesn't listen very well at all — a truth pastors face every Sunday!

New Wine — Old Skins

If television has so changed the style of communication for our people, how then do we preach to this audience? It doesn't work to serve the new wine of the gospel in the old skins of yesterday's communication style.

One of the problems is that the traditional education of pastors does not equip us to preach to a television audience. Quite the opposite. Education aims to make us good readers and writers, not oral communicators. Television is an oral, visual means of communication, but college, university and theological education is based on reading and writing. Lectures are basically written presentations read aloud, and we write down notes while listening. In our homework, we study our notes, read books, write papers and then take written tests. Except for occasional class discussions, communication in higher education is done through print. In today's schools the successful teachers are those with a long list of publications to their credit, not those who are skillful and imaginative as lecturers and teachers.

How different that is from ancient Greece, where rhetoric — public speaking, debate and discussion — was at the center of academic training! Rhetoric survived in the core curriculum of European universities well into the Renaissance years. Today however, classes in rhetoric can be held around a table in small seminar rooms, if indeed they are offered at all.

Particularly since the Gutenberg revolution of mass-produced books, orality has virtually died out of education. The advance of educational technology has pushed oral communication even further into the background — with plentiful paper, modern typewriters, computers which even correct your spelling and the ubiquitous copy machine. The picture of a typical student today is not the debating forum of ancient Greek academies, or even a student speaking with a teacher, but students sitting by themselves in front of a glowing screen typing more words a minute than Aristophanes and Sophocles, or even Charles Dickens and Mark Twain a century ago, could ever have imagined possible.

For centuries sermons have been carefully written essays of sound theology and logic which were read before the congregation. Good preachers spent a lot of time writing their sermons. Even when preachers don't write them out in full, they are prepared mentally as essays.

In this new age of communication skill in reading and writing is as indispensable as ever. Good preachers still write their sermons out. But as a form of oral communication, simply reading a well-crafted essay doesn't work in the pulpit anymore. Maybe it never did work as well as we would like to think!

The problem is that the standards of good writing are quite different from the norms of oral communication or television communication. A sermon might look splendid on paper, and it may be a superb sermon when one reads it silently, but it may not work at all from the pulpit. Too many fine sermons from a theological or pastoral viewpoint fall flat from the pulpit.

It has been said that wars are lost by the army which is still using the weapons of the previous war and won by the army which has figured out the next stage of new weapons. In the 1990s we are preaching to this television audience, but our sermons are crafted more for the reading audience of the 1890s. Richard Jensen speaks of the failure of "literate" churches to adapt to the new "post-literate" media age:

> *I believe the root of the crisis in the church is its failure to recognize and adapt to the quickly dawning world of electronic communication ... As the media changes, and as people are changed by the media, preaching must undergo significant change in order to communicate effectively.*[10]

We preachers may be working hard, but with the wrong medium.

The Rhetorical Challenge

On Sunday morning we find ourselves standing in front of people whose main form of communication is to watch electronic images on a screen. They are hungry for the good news of the gospel, but often it is not getting through to them. The heart of our ministry is communication, but we have ignored this massive change in communication media and continue to preach much the same way preachers have for centuries. It isn't working anymore. No wonder we're frustrated!

We have assumed that the basic task of preaching is sound theology. This is of course true, but today the rhetorical challenge is as important as the theological.

Must we capitulate to television and make our worship services as zippy as *Sesame Street* and our sermons as entertaining as a Jay Leno monologue? Can preaching be saved only by gimmickry? Is the age of preaching gone for good?

Not at all! There is now, and never will be, no substitute for the spoken word of preaching. To sell out to this new medium age and deliver sermons as frothy after-breakfast entertainment would be a shabby response to the magnificent calling of gospel preaching.

21

In spite of all the electronic wizardry of television, words are still what makes us human. The Christian Gospel cannot be communicated without them. Jesus is the Word of God made incarnate, and the good news of salvation needs words to be told. The true treasure of the church is still "the most holy gospel of the glory and grace of God," and it must still be spoken and heard to be conveyed.

Chapter 2
The TV Audience

Our sermon consumers are used to VCRs and Super Nintendo — strong visual images — they watch and then rewind. For our preaching, that certainly means it is a different generation of people out there listening. It has definite implications for what we say and how we say it.[11]
— Jerry L. Schmalenberger

I talk with many laypeople about sermons, and the comment I hear most often is: "Sermons are bo-o-o-oring!" This comment is of course not new in church history. Perhaps Eutychus thought the same thing about Paul's sermon, before he dozed off and fell out of the window. (Acts 20) Sermons in colonial America which droned on for two to three hours must have caused plenty of people to yawn and wonder when they could go home.

Today, however, television has lowered our boredom threshold way down. People are bored more easily and quickly today than ever before. Perceptions of sermons as boring are probably in direct ratio to the amount of time the listener watches television, videos or films.

Another comment one hears regularly is, "I thought the things the pastor said were interesting, but I can't remember now what the sermon was about." Preachers would be astonished to discover how many people cannot recall anything about the sermon by Sunday afternoon.

A New Audience

Preachers might be dismayed by these reactions, but they should not be surprised or baffled. It is clear that effective

23

communication is extremely complex, influenced by many factors:

- Good communication reaches the listener's emotions and will, not just the intellect.
- Much communication happens on a non-verbal level.
- The type of personality we are influences what and how we hear.
- Psychological factors and past experiences affect how we hear things.
- The left and right hemispheres of the brain hear and process information differently.
- The meanings of words change. Religious terms particularly may carry quite different messages to people in the same audience.

Noting that "our perceptions and understandings of the world are formed in far more complicated ways than merely by rational observation and judgment," Patricia Wilson-Kastner urges preachers to take into account these new insights.

> *We have become increasingly receptive to the enormous importance of our more intuitive side, to the centrality of the emotions, and to the way we express our awareness in images, pictures, and stories, which are all laden with feelings as well as intellectual assessments ... If we wish to be responsible preachers, then we need to appreciate and understand this brave new world we are entering, with its expanding consciousness of our very selves. Otherwise we run the risk of miscommunicating the Gospel instead of proclaiming it, or at least of missing some valuable media for sharing the good news of which we are stewards.*[12]

There are many factors producing this new audience, but the predominant influence is television. The television audience can be described with five characteristics, each one carrying clear implications for preaching.

1 — Television conveys pictures, not concepts.

Television transmits images; it is not suited to transmit a line of abstract thought or a logically developed argument.

That is done best in print. Television is basically a visual medium, and its dominance has made us a visual generation. Concepts and ideas might be talked about on television, but the primary impact is visual. People who prefer television over reading say, "In reading I don't see anything. On television I can both see and hear it." Television has the appeal of furnishing the whole picture ready-made for the audience.

People accustomed to television understand an idea or concept best if it is conveyed with an image or story — a visual picture in their mind illustrating the idea being conveyed. This is nothing new, since good speakers have always illustrated their message with concrete examples, but it is particularly true in the age of television.

Ideas are transmitted most effectively when they are communicated through and with visual imagery. The idea or doctrine of justification by grace cannot be easily transmitted on television. Watching someone explain it on the screen would send most viewers to the refrigerator. The suitable way to convey it on television would be to portray visually a person whose life and experience conveys what justification is and does. It does not work well to explain the doctrine of original sin on camera, even though various television dramas portray it very clearly!

Most of us preachers, however, are accustomed to preach by exposition, that is, we explain concepts and ideas. The television audience, however, understands ideas when they are not only explained but presented with language rich in visual imagery. That's why examples and illustrations are so important. They make the abstract concrete. From the words the mind pictures what's going on. When you listen to a radio drama or read a book, by the end of it you have created in your mind a vision of what the characters look like and how the scenery appears. The reason films of books are often unsatisfactory is that the people on screen don't look like we imagined them to be. We created a picture in our minds from the printed page.

As we shall see below, television as a visual medium has brought us back to the communication world of the Bible, where the message is so often presented in a richly visual fashion. The prophets, the psalmists, the Old Testament authors and Jesus himself communicated with images.

2 — Information is conveyed in bytes or impressions, rather than sequentially.

On the printed page ideas and thoughts are developed in logical sequence. Information is best conveyed by a step-by-step, coherent line of thought. A vast amount of information can be conveyed, more than the memory will retain, because one can always turn back and review what was written.

With television, however, people receive information not by sequence, but by impact and impression. Television messages are received by the brain as bytes, sight/sound images.

Automobile ads do not list pertinent specifications such as horsepower, consumer report tests, engine specifications, the grade of steel used and so forth. That is information which will be given in a printed description of the car. Within a fast 30 seconds a television ad bombards you not with relevant information but with glamorous images, flashing at you with split-second speed. The goal is not to educate you, but to leave your brain with an impression that you want this product.

Television advertisers use celebrities and gorgeous people, because they know such people make an impact on you even though your brain knows that the celebrity is just paid to make the ad and probably has never used the product. Nonetheless, the impression has been made in your subconscious.

We can become discouraged or cynical about the nature of television, but this new form of communication spills over into how people listen to sermons.

Perhaps in the past congregations expected and were able to follow a lengthy, logical development of thought in a sermon. Many of the great sermons in the past presented a well-reasoned, logically developed line of thought. They were splendid essays, written down in full and read from the pulpit. Preachers with good theological education tend to be good at analyzing and explaining, but a sermon needs more than that to put the message across.

People are no less logical or intelligent than in the past, but a lengthy, logically developed string of thoughts puts them to sleep. The message of salvation in Jesus Christ can be as powerfully conveyed with sound theology today as in the past, but it must be done by bytes, the key paragraphs or elements which will grab the listener's mind and stick in the memory. Without them, people will think back on the sermon and reflect, "The pastor said a lot of interesting things, but I really don't know what the sermon was about." That person is really saying, "During the sermon I thought good things were being said, but nothing in particular grabbed me." There were no central bytes which the listener remembered, around which the content of the sermon stuck in the brain.

Of course a sermon must be logically and cohesively developed, and it must include information about the text and interpretation of the text. But the sermon must include bytes that grab people's attention and stick in their memory. Recalling these highlights, listeners will remember the ideas, thoughts and information in the sermon.

This is not new. Throughout church history good preachers have done this by instinct, including in their sermon key phrases, imagery or illustrations which have served as such bytes. Read the great preachers of the past. They may have lived in a print age, but their sermons always included powerful and colorful images, which made a deep impact on their listeners. Television forces us to do what good preachers have always done.

3 — Our concentration span is shorter.

Commercial television has accustomed us to brief intermissions every 10-12 minutes, if not sooner. We expect frequent snack or bathroom breaks. Movie producers become nervous if their film directors go beyond two hours, and they know that it will take dramatic action on screen to hold audience attention beyond that limit.

From historical accounts of public speaking in the past, we can assume that people paid attention longer than they do

27

now. The format for the 1858 debates between Abraham Lincoln and Stephen Douglas, for instance, was three hours in length. The first speaker spoke for an hour; the second speaker had an hour and a half, leaving the first speaker 30 minutes for rebuttal. Compare that with the television format for presidental debates today, where a speaker is given two minutes to explain a Middle East policy or a plan for economic recovery! In the television age candidates know that a catchy 30-second television spot on the evening news is worth more than a carefully worked out speech.

Kate Moody examined the effect of television on young children and observed:

> *Experienced teachers, those who have taught long enough to know several generations of children, are coming to alarming conclusions about current learning styles and abilities: Kids can't listen for any length of time ... they can't pay attention ("When I read them stories out loud, they squirm and say, 'I can't hear it without pictures.' ") ...* [13]

How long should today's sermons be? That depends on the preacher and the expectations of the congregation. With the television generation the age of the one-hour sermon is past. Even the traditional 20-minute length is longer than today's average sermon. Many sermons I hear are too long and would improve with pruning. Very seldom do I leave church wishing the preacher would have said more about the topic. The answer to sermon length is: Deliver your message as well as possible, then sit down!

Sermon length isn't the real issue. The crucial question is: Are there elements in the sermon which will arrest and hold the audience's attention? If they're not there, people will drift off mentally to study the stained-glass windows, count rows of bricks, or fill in the os and es in the bulletins. Good preachers constantly ask themselves, "What is there in this sermon that will keep, or recapture, the people's attention?"

4 — We listen more passively.

With the speaker on the screen before us, television might look more personal than the printed page, but that is not the case. When people speak to us personally, we pay attention out of courtesy. If somebody is talking to you, it would be rude to reach over, pick up a magazine and start reading. In the midst of a conversation it would be impolite to get up without a word and head to the refrigerator for a snack.

With television, however, we have become accustomed to doing that regularly, and the television speaker doesn't mind at all! Most of us do all sorts of things while people talk to us on television — knit, read the paper, cook, wash dishes, write letters or whatever.

The electronic medium has produced a passive audience. We are used to listening with half an ear, easily distracted.

Translate this to church, and we have people in the pews who listen for a few minutes, then think about something else. Their minds wander about for a few minutes, until they get back on track with the sermon.

One of the results of passive listening is superficial listening. Because we do not have to give total attention to the person on television, we listen with half an ear. Young people who have grown up in a multi-media culture insist they can do this very effectively. They work on their homework in front of the television, perhaps with a phone propped up on one ear talking to a friend.

One can debate how well we listen with other distractions going on, but the fact is that people can be looking attentively at the pastor and their minds are a million miles away.

Preachers have an advantage over television: We are there, personally, in front of the audience. With the tendency toward passive and superficial listening so ingrained in the television audience, they will listen, but only if they sense that they are being addressed directly and personally. Again and again I hear the comment from laypersons: "I wish our pastor would talk to us directly rather than reading the sermon!"

29

At the first sign that the speaker's main focus is on the manuscript rather than the people, today's listeners tune out. Professionals in public speaking know that. Television speakers instinctively know that their presence in the room is only electronic, not personal, and they know that it becomes even more impersonal if they read. So they use teleprompters to give the illusion of not reading. If a network newscaster kept looking down at a manuscript, the ratings of that channel would drop out of sight.

The television audience becomes passive and inattentive very quickly if the pastor does not speak to them directly. There are ways of combining careful preparation of a manuscript with effective delivery, which will be discussed below.

Pastors also need to be intentional in capturing people's attention — whether it's using a story or illustration, using one's voice dramatically, or taking a dramatic turn in the flow of the sermon. There are ways of jarring an inattentive audience to attention, and we need to use them.

5 — Television is a combination of verbal and non-verbal communication.

There is a profound difference in how communication through television compares with communication through the printed page. How an author looks or speaks is not a factor in reading. The printed page is well-suited for serious discussion precisely because the personalities of the authors do not distract from the topics being discussed.

Television is different. We hear and see who is speaking. When people speak on the screen, the impact of their words is inseparable from the listener's perception of them as persons. The politician who appears on TV and pleads, "Let's stick with the issues in this campaign and leave personalities out of it," does not understand the reality of television.

This works two ways. On one hand the audience senses a credibility as they hear and see something. A speaker who conveys sincerity and conviction will be believed more than a person who is nervous and unsure, even though they may be speaking the very same words. On the other hand, television has also produced a wide-spread skepticism. We are impressed by a smooth speaker who oozes charm. Yet our instincts lead us to think twice. Using gorgeous people to advertise cosmetics and cars catches our attention, but we know they probably never use what they advertise.

The fact that through electronic communication we both hear and see the speakers works to the church's favor in the long run. The parish pastor preaches not as an impersonal performer from a distant studio, nor as words on pages of paper, but as a real person with the audience. Furthermore — this is the deep dynamic of pastoral ministry — the message carries credibility not only because the speaking is immediate, but because the one preaching is the same person who calls on us when we are sick, teaches our children, visits our shut-in grandparents and listens when we have problems. No television personality can begin to match the close bond between the preacher and the audience!

The Perspective

When we examine the effect television has on an audience, our first impulse might be to become discouraged. We are using simple speech to convey a message to people who are accustomed to more than speech. How can we communicate by speaking to people who are used to learning by television?

Simply put, we need to see our preaching from the perspective of our listeners — put ourselves in their eyes, their minds, their ears. Donald Macleod describes our audience this way:

> *Before the preacher every Sunday morning are several hundred wandering minds with diverse and fleeting foci ... Remember their attention response and span are influenced and determined by watching and hearing six weekdays of television commercials ... More often than*

*not they sit back in the pews, fold their spiritual arms,
and say within themselves, "Well, what have you got to
say this morning that will interest me?"*[14]

Once we understand the television audience and keep its characteristics constantly in mind as we prepare and preach, people will hear what is being said, and this great and wonderful Gospel of Life will enter powerfully into people's hearts and lives.

The challenge of television compels us to be better preachers. Since the rhetoric of television is in part a restoration of oral communication, our preaching will become more "oral" in nature. This also means that we will be drawn increasingly to the Bible as the chief resource for our preaching, because the Bible was written to an oral society, and its communication style is primarily oral.

Chapter 3

Words As Images

... we are addressing a generation accustomed to acting primarily on visual stimuli ... In our modern age the preacher must therefore translate the biblical message into one that awakens all the senses, into words that cause a congregation also to see and feel and smell and taste. Otherwise the people listening may never hear the words in which the gospel is framed.[15]
— Elizabeth Achtemeier

The printed word communicates by a line of thought. Television communicates by images. Clearly we must use language rich with visual imagery. Furthermore, today we understand that effective communication must involve the whole person, not just the intellect, but also the emotions and the will. We want not only to explain, but to move, to inspire and to motivate. That can be done only with vivid and colorful language. This has always been true, but television has made it crystal clear.

Imagery As Life Itself

The reason that imagery works is that we live our lives in the concrete, and the use of imagery forces us to connect our sermons to daily life. Jerry Schmalenberger urges preachers to "keep your sermon close to the ground ... We must deal with the nitty gritty issues of the day in everyday language."[16]

Fred B. Craddock, professor of preaching and New Testament at the Chandler School of Theology in Atlanta, Georgia, advocates an "inductive movement" in preaching, beginning with the lives and situation of the people in the pews, then moving to the biblical message, rather than stating a general truth and deducing particular applications:

> *The plain fact of the matter is that we are seeking to communicate with people whose experiences are concrete. Everyone lives inductively, not deductively. No farmer deals with the problem of calfhood, only with the calf .... The minister says, "all men are mortal" and meets drowsy agreement; he announces that "Mr. Brown's son is dying," and the church becomes the church.*[17]

Imagery takes an abstract, general idea and expresses it with a concrete, specific term which creates a picture in the mind. For example, "Flowers are beautiful" is a true statement, but the word flower is a generic word and creates no picture in your mind unless your imagination narrows the term down and creates for itself a picture in your mind. However, if I say, "Roses are beautiful," that's more specific, because we know what a rose looks like and the image comes to mind. If I say, "Red roses are beautiful," that becomes even more specific. But if I say, "See that red rose on the table? Isn't it gorgeous?" I have brought the idea of flowers down to one specific flower. You know exactly what I'm talking about because you can see it.

In preaching a sermon on Matthew 5:44, "Love your enemies ...,"one could explain how Christians love even our enemies because God has loved us while we were yet sinners and Jesus sacrificed himself on the cross to atone for our sins and reconcile us to a merciful God, and so on. That is true, and it needs to be said. But it's abstract. What the sermon needs is an example of a person who had reason to hate somebody, but whose hatred was turned to love through the presence and example of Jesus. That image would illustrate for the listener what is meant with the text. In this television age the preacher should always ask, "This idea or truth which I want to communicate — what image can I use to fix it in the listener's mind?"

34

The power of imagery in words is nothing new. Poets have always known it. Indeed, that's what poetry is. For example, in analyzing the sense of futility a person might feel about life, one could say,

> "Many people feel a sense of futility about life, thinking that it has no purpose. They live day by day, but their life lacks meaning."

That is true, but it is stated abstractly. The words in themselves carry no imagery and a congregation's eyes would soon glaze over with this kind of general talk, even though it is all theologically correct and true.

Shakespeare said the same thing. After scratching his way to the throne, Macbeth learns of his wife's death and is filled with foreboding that all his murderous plotting will backfire. In his despair he says,

> Tomorrow, and tomorrow, and tomorrow,
> Creeps in this petty pace from day to day,
> To the last syllable of recorded time;
> And all our yesterdays have lighted fools
> The way to dusty death. Out, out, brief candle!
> Life's but a walking shadow, a poor player
> That struts and frets his hour up on the stage
> And then is heard no more: it is a tale
> Told by an idiot, full of sound and fury,
> Signifying nothing.[18]

This description is lush with imagery. Every line creates pictures in the mind. Combine an abstract, general statement with imagery like this (although 10 lines of such richness would be too much all at once for most listeners), and your message will have impact. The listener's mind has been given imagery which illustrates what you're saying.

Walter Brueggemann, Professor of Old Testament at Columbia Seminary in Decatur, Georgia, is alarmed that the gospel has become "a truth that has been flattened, trivialized and rendered inane," that is, it has been reduced to bland familiarity by people who have heard it so often. The only possibility for the renewal of preaching is that we become "poets that speak against a prose world."

> *The task and possibility of preaching is to open out the good news of the gospel with alternative modes of speech — speech that is dramatic, artistic, capable of inviting persons to join in another conversation, free of the reason of technique, encumbered by ontologies that grow abstract, unembarrassed about concreteness.*[19]

Richard Jensen goes a step further and argues for a "paradigm shift" in preaching from "thinking in ideas," characteristic of a literate print culture, to "thinking in story."[20]

Good speakers have always spoken with color and imagination by instinct.[21] But in today's age of visual communication it has become doubly crucial for preachers to create concrete pictures in the minds of their listeners.

Biblical Imagery

Long before television, the Hebrews used pictorial language. They thought in metaphor and image. The Old Testament is a treasure house of images. The Old Testament narrative itself is a story, the account of the Jewish people from Adam on through the story of the divided kingdom.

One of the most effective uses of imagery in the Bible was Nathan's confrontation with David. The prophet could have come to the king and exposed his sin by saying, "You have sent Uriah to his death so that you could take his wife Bathsheba for yourself!" Rather he stood before the king and told a story, "There were two men in a certain city, the one rich and the other poor ..." (2 Samuel 12:1) David was drawn into the story, so that when it was turned to him he immediately grasped the meaning. In writing about the use of stories in sermons, William Bausch first considered titling his book *Nathan's Legacy,* because all preachers:

stand in Nathan's tradition. He, the rest of the prophets, and in fact all the sacred writers . . . thought and wrote in terms of stories.[22]

Take any psalm and "translate" it into the clear but abstract prose we usually use. Then compare how bland it is compared to the original. Look at some well-known verses from Psalm 139 for example:

Plain Prose
How can I get away from God?
    Can I get away from
      his presence?
No matter where I go,
    you are there.
You will always guide me
      and take care of me, no
      matter how far I
      might go.
You can see everything,
      so darkness doesn't
      hide me from you.

Psalmist's Version
Where can I go from your spirit?
    Or where can I flee from your
      presence?
If I ascend to heaven, you are
      there;
    if I make my bed in Sheol, you
      are there;
If I take the wings of the morning
    and settle at the farthest
      limits of the sea,

even there your hand shall
    lead me,
and your right hand shall hold
    me fast.
If I say, "Surely the darkness
    shall cover me,
and the light around me become
    night,"
even the darkness is not dark to
    you;
the night is as bright as the
    day,
for darkness is as light to you.

The message of the two readings is the same, but the plain prose, stripped of its imagery, is colorless and bland. One can do the same thing with any of the psalms. Imagine how Psalm 24 would sound as abstract statements, without its imagery of the shepherd, the valley, the table, and so on!

The Old Testament was written when oral communication was predominant. In the New Testament the language and thought of Jesus, the disciples and others were formed by their Hebrew background. Jesus' entire communication was oral. Except for the single instance when he wrote in the sand (John 8:6, 8), Jesus never wrote a word, and even in John 8 we don't know what he wrote. In speaking with people, he knew the power of imagery. When he was criticized for eating with sinners and tax collectors, he could have responded by explaining, "God considers everybody precious and receives even the worst sinners with mercy and forgiveness when they come to him." That would have been correct, but abstract. Rather Jesus responded, "There was a man who had two sons; and the younger of them said to his father, 'Father, give me the share of the property that falls to me ...'" (Luke 15:11f.) Immediately an image comes to mind of a father with an impatient son itching for independence. As the story unfolds, we watch in our mind's eye as the younger son goes off into the far

38

country, squanders his inheritance, returns with anxiety only to see his father rush out and lift him off his feet with a hug.

The story of the Prodigal Son, or the Waiting Father, is so powerful that it is one of the best known and loved passages in the whole Bible. Few people then or now would have noticed or remembered Jesus' answer if it had been expressed abstractly. Everybody remembers his story of the father and his two sons.

Kinds Of Imagery

There are various kinds of imagery, from full-blown stories to a single word which evokes a picture in the mind. We use metaphors and similes regularly in our everyday language. A metaphor is an image in place of an abstract term. In describing King Herod Jesus could have said, "Herod is a cunning and untrustworthy man," which was correct but colorless. Instead he called Herod a fox, an image which conveyed immediately exactly what he meant.

Jesus used metaphors repeatedly. How did he express his love for Jerusalem? "How often would I have gathered your children together as a hen gathers her brood under her wings . . . !" (Matthew 23:37)

"Beware of false prophets," he warned his followers, "who come to you in sheep's clothing but inwardly are ravenous wolves." (Matthew 7:15)

A simile is a comparison usually stated with like or as. Something is like something else, and immediately an image is produced in our mind. Listen again to Jesus:

"The kingdom of heaven is like treasure . . . Again, the kingdom is like a merchant in search of fine pearls . . . Again, the kingdom of heaven is like a net which was thrown into the sea . . ." (Matthew 13:44f)

"Woe to you, scribes and Pharisees, hypocrites! for you are like whitewashed tombs, which outwardly appear beautiful, but within they are full of dead men's bones and all uncleanness." (Matthew 23:27)

39

Parables are also the language of imagery. The definition of a parable often used for children is "an earthly story with a heavenly meaning." That's an everyday way of saying, "an image from life to express an abstract or spiritual meaning." Every one of Jesus' parables combine a vivid image with a meaning.

The most effective imagery is that which speaks directly about human life, particularly those situations which touch the listener personally. When we hear the parable of the Prodigal Son, we cannot help but think about our own fathers, our own past and our own feelings in the reaction of the elder brother. When a pastor tells a story about a person struggling with illness, everybody in the congregation who has experienced similar suffering is immediately drawn into the story.

Colorful Language

"Imagery" can be broadly defined as colorful language. Academic education trains us to write with economy and accuracy. Speaking needs much more. In preaching class I tell students, "In your past years of education and here in your other classes, you are trained to be precise, accurate, banal and boring. Here we try to change all that." That's exaggerated, but it makes the point. To touch and move an audience, a preacher must shift from the abstract language of the classroom to language rich in imagery for the pulpit.

We need to become adventuresome, even daring and exciting in our speech. Good preaching needs language with vigor, muscle, energy and punch. In short, we need language with the rich texture of imagery — metaphor, simile, story, zippy adjectives and verbs.

Be a poet in the pulpit, not a bureaucrat or professor. When Professor Brueggemann urges preachers to become poets, he is talking of language with verve and muscle:

By poetry, I do not mean rhyme, rhythm, or meter, but language that moves like Bob Gibson's fast ball, that

*jumps at the right moment, that breaks open old worlds
with surprise abrasion, and pace. Poetic speech is the only
proclamation worth doing in a situation of reductionism,
the only proclamation, I submit, that is worthy of the
name preaching.*[23]

The impact of colorful language is not new to the modern
age. Guest speakers and preachers have always been poets in
their speech. Read the banal, prosy statements listed first and
compare that with the vigorous, image-filled language of the
great preachers of the past:

Flat Speech

1 — One should pray to become closer to God, not just
to get good things from God.

2 — Jesus looked like an ordinary man, even a fisher-
man of his times, and he knew he would die; even then
he told us our redemption was near.

3 — God is pleased with creative preaching, just as God
was pleased at creation and Easter. The devil doesn't want
the Word preached well, because then his reign would
be threatened.

Colorful Speech

1 — Whoever has decided to pray, really to pray, must
seize the hand of God, not the pennies in his hand.[24]

2 — Christ himself was fantastic with his hair every which-
way and smelling of fish and looking probably a lot more
like Groucho Marx than like Billy Budd as he stood there
with his ugly death already thick as flies about him and
said to raise our heads, raise our heads for Christ's sake,
because our redemption is near.[25]

3 — The Author of the text laughs in delight, the way that Author has laughed only at creation and at Easter, but laughs again when the sermon carries the day against the prose of the Dark Prince who wants no new poetry in the region he thinks he governs. Where the poetry is sounded, the Prince knows a little of the territory has been lost to its true Ruler.[26]

My faculty colleague James Nestingen preached a sermon on Matthew 14:22-36, the story of Peter walking on the water toward Jesus, then sinking when he began worrying about the waves rather than keeping his eyes on Jesus. This could be explained in clear prose:

> *We also can be distracted by the anxieties and worries surrounding us, taking our attention away from Jesus.*

Instead he said:

> *A lot of us are sopping wet up to our knees. Others are soaking wet up to the belt line, even the shoulders. And some of us are barely holding our heads above water, wondering if we'll make it at all!*

That's imagery. It's the difference between explaining something abstractly or saying the same thing in language which will produce a vivid picture in the listener's mind.

If somebody asks the listener on Monday what the sermon was about, the first thing that will come to mind is a person sinking in panic into the whitecaps. The memory of that image will help the person reflect back to the text, then to the theme and the explanation of the sermon. For a person conditioned by television the impact is made by the imagery of the language.

A "Controlling Image"

Robert Hughes, president of Lutheran Seminary of Philadelphia and long-time teacher of preachers, recommends

42

what he calls a "controlling image" as the heart of a sermon.

> *These images, usually introduced at the outset of the sermon, come back again and again and give unity to the sermon.*[27]

He suggests "framing" the sermon with such an image, where it recurs at the beginning and end of the sermon, thus fixing it in the listener's mind and providing the unity to the sermon.

If a preacher is using colorful language, a sermon will have many images as it moves along. The danger is clutter. There must be a sense of unity in the sermon, and this is done by making sure that the listener knows what the primary theme, or "controlling image," is. Patricia Wilson-Kastner advises,

> *Normally we will want to make one particular image central; other images will either clarify or support it. Sometimes another major image will appear along with or support the primary image in a sermon. Sometimes these other images find their places as deliberate contrasts to the primary image ... The key to the integrity of the sermon is the underlying ... unity of its imagery.*[28]

The key is to look at the sermon and ask yourself, "When the listener thinks back on this sermon, what idea or picture will stand out as the 'glue' that holds it all together?" It may be a story, illustration, image, or the text itself. When you decide what it is, then ask, "Have I made this unifying theme clear throughout the flow of the whole sermon?"

I was preparing a sermon one summer week on Matthew 10:34-42 (Cycle A, Pentecost 6), where Jesus warns the disciples of the controversy and distress they will encounter as they spread his word into the world. "I have not come to bring peace, but a sword," he warns them. The Old Testament lesson was Jeremiah 28:5-9, where the false prophet Hananiah sugarcoats Jeremiah's stern warnings by assuring the people of peace.

I wanted to contrast the powerful effect of Jesus' words with the innocuous pabulum our society has often made of the biblical message, that "gospel of good feelings" with a kindly, harmless God who loves us but doesn't bother us much. I needed an image which would convey banality. I chose muzak, that travesty of music which businesses use to soothe people into feeling good. It was a perfect image to contrast the power of the gospel and Jesus' warning to his disciples. People would immediately picture themselves in stores, offices or elevators where this "grocery music" is playing, as my children call it. The film *The Sound Of Music* was popular at the time, so I used a play on words and titled the sermon, *The Sound Of Muzak.*

The entire sermon contrasted muzak, which is not meant to be listened to but only to soothe, with the gospel, which has power, and which upsets lives as well as heals them. I conducted no surveys following the service, but if the sermon was effective, people who were asked about the sermon would reflect back and think,

> *"Well, let's see now, the pastor talked about muzak, which is harmless noise, and, yes, that's different than the message of Jesus, which can turn lives upside down ... In the text Jesus warned us the gospel was strong medicine."*

Muzak became the controlling image, around which the whole sermon revolved. That image would capture the listeners' attention and stick in their memory, and from that impact they could recall the message of the sermon.[29]

The Image And The Message

If you use an image which has a strong visual impact, it must fit exactly with the point of your sermon. Otherwise people will remember the image but be distracted from the message of the text itself, which should always be the heart of the sermon.

I recently heard a sermon on Luke 15, the Prodigal Son (Cycle C, Lent 4), where the pastor told a moving story about a college girl who messed up her life in a morass of alcohol, drugs and broken friendships. She became so despondent that she took her own life. Her parents, who would have joyfully accepted her back home in spite of her failings, were heartbroken.

The story did not fit the text — in fact was the direct opposite of the text. It was the story of someone who died without coming home, who never knew the gracious welcome of the father. The impact of the sermon was not on the joy of homecoming, nor on the accepting love of the parents, but upon the tragedy of the girl. Her misery overwhelmed the sermon. In fact, the pastor was still grieving the loss of a college girl in his previous congregation, and had allowed the powerful feeling of his own grief to dictate the sermon.

It was a memorable sermon, because the story was powerful in itself, but it was not a sermon on the Prodigal Son. Rather than reinforcing and illustrating the text, the story had buried the message of the text. The sermon belonged to a different text.

Stories And Illustrations

Story sermons and narrative preaching are currently very popular. Stories in sermons have always been popular, but this is doubly true in the television age, because stories produce images in the mind. Every preacher has experienced it: As we explain something, we note the mother in the back pew digging through her purse for crayons and a snack to quiet the squirrely child, the teenager counting bricks on the wall or passing notes to friends, the head nodding up and down, and so on. Then begin a story and the whole congregation becomes hushed and attentive. Finish the story and the activity resumes.

Some of the discussion about story or narrative preaching is unhelpful. For instance, some say a story should never be explained, but should be allowed to speak for itself. That's not the real issue. One can tell a story with no further explanation. One can also give the story a context at the beginning, as with the parable of the Prodigal Son (Luke 15:1-2), add an explanation at the end, or both, as with the parable of the Good Samaritan. (Luke 10:25-29, 36-37) One tells a story to convey a message, and the test of its effectiveness is if the story works to convey that message.

On the other hand, one can kill a story by over-explaining what the audience has already grasped. How much we explain about a story will depend on the audience, and a preacher will have to determine how best to put the message across. "Our goal is not to tell good stories," advises Richard Jensen. "Our goal is to communicate the biblical story through our use of story."[30]

Some practical guidelines in the use of illustrations and stories in sermons are:

- Tell enough, but don't include extra details to clutter up the point.

- Put it in the right place. A deeply moving story told at the beginning of the sermon tends to overshadow anything said afterward.

- Make sure it's accurate. I once heard a preacher tell Dostoevski's story from *Brothers Karamazov* of Raskalnikov's rebirth in prison after receiving the New Testament. It's a splendid illustration, but it's in *Crime and Punishment.*

- Never divulge confidences or tell stories from your ministry which cause people to wonder who you're talking about.

- Stories of your own experiences give instant credibility to your sermon. On the other hand, avoid repeated stories of yourself and your own family, particularly if they make you the hero or the goat, or embarrass your children.

God In The World

The use of colorful language, imagery and stories in preaching is really a matter of good theology. Preachers who believe that God is truly at work in the world and in people's lives constantly see connections between the gospel and life around them. They become attuned to see meaning and significance in what they see every day, and those concrete images and examples find their way into sermons.

Chapter 4

Structure And Clarity

I understand the stories the pastor told and thought they were interesting, but I couldn't see how the sermon fit together.

— A 15-year-old's comment during
the writing of this book

Many sermons with good material fall flat simply because the audience doesn't follow the flow of the message. With today's audience listening superficially with a short attention span, there are some basic principles one can use so that the sermon will be (a) heard, (b) understood and (c) remembered.

Our View And Their View

One problem is that we preachers think of our sermons in a wholly different way than the audience, in two respects:

(1) During the week we spend a lot of time thinking about our sermons. We study the text, think about it throughout the week, mull over themes, and often go to sleep thinking about what we'll say. By Sunday morning the sermon is so much a part of us that we know exactly what we want to say and how everything fits together.

How different that is from the people in the pews, who sit back in their pews after the gospel reading with no idea at all what the pastor is going to talk about. When we begin preaching, the sermon is second nature to us; the audience starts from scratch with no idea at all what is coming.

49

(2) Related to that is the obvious difference between print and oral communication, which we tend to overlook: With print communication we can always look back over what we've read, but with oral communication we hear it once, and there's no going back. We have worked with our sermon manuscript for hours and know exactly what's there. The listener in the congregation, on the other hand, comes wholly unprepared, hears it once, and it's gone.

When the 15-year-old cited above was listening to the sermon, the pastor knew exactly what he was trying to say, and exactly how the components of the sermon fit together. No doubt he had spent hours in preparation, and the message was crystal clear in his mind. The sermon was biblical and relevant to the lives of the listeners.

Had the pastor heard the comment of the 15-year-old cited above, he would have been astonished. He would assume that the young man had not listened too well. After all, the pastor knew exactly what he was saying and how it fit together.

In this case, however, the youth had listened and could recall parts of the sermon. But the sermon had lacked focus and impact, so that the over-all effect was diffuse. There were some good ideas but no bytes that stuck in his mind, no pegs which grabbed his attention and around which the message took shape and focus. The sermon was like a pudding which was once served to Winston Churchill. It tasted good, the prime minister said, but "it lacked a theme."

Preachers can improve their preaching a great deal by constantly looking at their sermons as the congregation will hear them.

"It Didn't Fit Together"

Wondering "how it all fit together" or "what was the pastor getting at" is a common reaction I've heard from many laypeople. There are two reasons for this.

1 — Too Many Ideas.

The sermon didn't fit together, because there were too many ideas in it, one of the most common problems in preaching. We might have a good theme in mind on Tuesday, but by Thursday we have added other good ideas and illustrations. Having thought about it for hours, it is very clear to us how it all fits together. Maybe even while delivering the sermon we think of another interesting item and lob that into the sermon as we're preaching.

Then we are surprised to discover that there were people in the pews who left church wondering what the real point of the sermon was about. If 20 people had written down a one-sentence summary of the sermon, you would have received 20 different summaries!

One huge problem in preaching to a television audience is that we cover way too much ground in a sermon. It is a carry-over from the habits of print. In good writing one tries to convey as much information as economically as possible. A writer can include side comments, related ideas and peripheral information, because the reader can constantly look back and refresh her memory on what has been said. A sermon is heard just once, and too many ideas produce a cluttered sermon.

2 — Unclear Connections.

There may have been a main theme, but the various parts of the sermon were not well connected to each other, and transitions from section to section were not clearly made. What was very clear in the pastor's mind was not conveyed to the audience.

With today's shortened attention span, a person listens for a few minutes, then finds his mind wandering. No doubt this has happened to you as a listener, too. When you come back on track with the sermon, you wonder, "How did the preacher get *there*?" You wonder how this paragraph relates to what was said five minutes ago. If you were reading the sermon, you could look back and see. In preaching it's once through and gone.

Faced with listeners who tend to listen superficially and passively, the preacher has to make doubly sure "it all fits together!"

A Main Theme

In communicating to this new audience it is absolutely essential to:
(1) have a central, main theme;
(2) make sure that all parts of the sermon are clearly related to the main theme.
Without a main point around which the whole sermon revolves, listeners will come away with all sorts of diffuse ideas on what the sermon is about, with no idea on how it's all connected. That kind of preaching is like the terrible definition I once heard of preaching which is unfortunately often true:

> *"Preaching is like throwing a bucket of water at a case full of empty pop bottles. A little will go into every bottle. It won't be much, and it will be a different spoonful in every bottle."*

Of course people hear different things in a sermon, and the part of a sermon which hits one person will be different with somebody else. But it's a definition of poor preaching, because it suggests the preacher need only spray out a jumble of ideas like a lawn sprinkler. Such preaching will be diffuse and accidental.

One of my neighbors in a previous parish was a splendid pastor, but whenever I met him during the week and asked what he was going to preach about, his answer was the same, "Well, I have a few ideas I'm going to throw out." Unfortunately that's exactly what he did, seldom narrowing his good ideas to one focus and usually getting in as many as possible. They were good ideas, and no doubt some landed on target and affected people's lives. But the overall impression of his people was similar to the 15-year-old: "I never saw how it all fit together." His ministry was accomplished through superb weekday pastoral care, without much reinforcement from effective Sunday preaching.

One test of an effective sermon is what a listener answers when asked, "What was the sermon about?" If the sermon has an underlying unity, the listener will answer by summarizing that main theme. From that core the listener can recreate the other elements of the sermon which reinforced or illustrated the main point. In his usual colorful way, Charles Haddon Spurgeon, the great English preacher of the last century, advised, "One tenpenny nail driven home and clenched will be more useful than a score of tin-tacks loosely fixed, to be pulled out again in an hour."[31]

How can you, the preacher, know when you have arrived at a main point? The first thing necessary is that you know what you are trying to say and can summarize the sermon's main point in a sentence or two. The central theme of the sermon is the plant which has grown from your study, prayer and reflection on the biblical text. The text itself is the root of the main theme, forming and shaping what you will say about it.

Boiling Down The Ideas

As you think about and work on the sermon during the week, various ideas come to mind. I find it helpful to jot down these ideas, and I end up with a list of a whole lot of disparate ideas which will require drastic pruning before the finished product. For example, I am working on a sermon for the ordination of one of our students. The gospel lesson is Luke 7:1-10, Jesus' healing of the Roman centurion's slave. It's a magnificent text for an ordination of one who will preach the gospel, because of all people the Roman officer understands the power of words. Feeling unworthy of a visit from Jesus, he sends friends to ask Jesus simply to speak the word of healing. "For I am a man set under authority, with soldiers under me," he says, "and I say to one, 'Go,' and he goes; and to another, 'Come,' and he comes." Jesus marvels, for this man truly has faith in Jesus' words!

Over a couple weeks my list of scattered ideas for this sermon looked like this:

- The contempt our society has for the spoken word, expressed in such proverbs as "I'll believe it when I see it," "A picture is worth a thousand words," "Talk is cheap," or in the most foolish of all such proverbs, "Sticks and stones may break my bones, but words will never hurt me!"

- Today's idea of words "representing something," versus the biblical idea of words carrying within themselves the power or thing expressed, such as God's speech at creation, or Jesus' words in healing.

- Similar miracles of Jesus, where his word conveyed power, and this section of Luke is brimming with such wonderful stories — the raising of the widow of Nain's son, 7:11-17; the woman anointing his feet, 7:36-50; the parable of the sower, 8:1-15; the stilling of the storm, 8:22-25; the Gerasene demon, 8:26-33, all examples of the power of Jesus' word.

- Instances from real life where words are important, such as "I love you," "I hate you," . . .

- The pain of somebody not even speaking to you.

- From Dostoevsky's *Crime And Punishment*, the story of how the convicted murderer Raskalnikov's life was renewed with the New Testament given him as he went to prison, and how the reading of the Lazarus story was the beginning of his rebirth.

- The expectation people have as they come to church on Sunday to hear the life-giving words of salvation.

There are a lot of good ideas here, and one could rattle them all off in 20 minutes, like a machine gun spitting out a barrage of good thoughts.

Settling On The Central Theme

Good preparation will produce far too many ideas for one sermon. The most difficult task of sermon preparation for me is to narrow it all down to one central theme.

Donald Macleod suggests first writing down ideas as you "brood" about the text, then jotting down more ideas as you study commentaries. Following that, with the two worksheets of ideas in front of you, "begin another brooding session." If one does this preparation carefully, the sermon theme will emerge:

> *Suddenly — sometimes early, sometimes late — there comes the moment of illumination, the aha! experience. Out of the collage of notations, an idea leaps at you, arresting you, and becomes the Word of God to and for you, the fruit of your prayerful insight into truth in your solitary thrust with scripture. Immediately start "Worksheet 3" and at the top of the page state in one succinct sentence this central idea which will be the integrating theme of the sermon and the pivotal point around which your message will take its shape.*[32]

The main point must finally communicate the point of the text and move into the lives of the people. H. Grady Davis lists four characteristics of a good sermon idea:

1. It must be narrow enough to be sharp.
2. It must have in it a force that is expanding, reaching out in different directions, exploding ... fermenting.
3. It must be true.
4. It must be loaded with the realities of the human heart.[33]

Perhaps the hardest part of the process is the next one: All those other interesting ideas, which turned out to be not related to the main theme, are tucked back into the drawers of your mind, or into the file folders in your office, for later use. The main theme controls the sermon from now on. All the components of the sermon must be related to that central thought. From that focus outward we begin putting the sermon together.

Arranging The Pieces

Once you have decided on the central message of the sermon, you will have already thought of some of the other components related to the main theme, such as:

- how the text conveys the message
- examples of how this has worked in today's lives
- how the sinful world has rejected the biblical message, including examples
- problems of interpretation, or questions people might have about the text, and so forth.

As you arrange these pieces, keep putting yourself in the place of the listener, who will hear the sermon once through, and that with maybe only half an ear. When a listener is asked after lunch, "What was the sermon about?" what do you hope she will answer? Have you made it so clear that she will get it? Will she remember that central point and summarize it? Will she then remember other parts of the sermon — explanation, hookup to the text, examples, etc. — and connect them with the main theme?

The listener may recall the main theme by remembering a story, or a controlling image. The text itself, if you have retold it creatively, may carry the main theme.

Another way of checking for your main point is to ask yourself, "When the sermon is finished, what will stick in the listener's mind?" Then in the delivery make clear to the audience that this is the heart of the sermon. Pastor Stanley Olson, my partner at First Lutheran Church in Duluth, Minnesota, and I had our confirmation students take sermon notes, writing down the main theme of the sermon. Each fall he would show the new students how to do it. One of the frustrating parts of doing sermon notes is to read them afterward and realize how often these junior high youth fail to get the point of the sermon. On one occasion Stan paused in his sermon, leaned over the pulpit and said, "Now for you confirmation students writing sermon summaries, write *this* down as the main point of the sermon," and then he stated the heart of the sermon. The students wrote it down, but of course the rest of the congregation got it too.

One cannot be so blunt every Sunday, but the sermon must be delivered in such a way that there is a focus on the central message and that the congregation will know it.

Three-Point Sermon

The traditional three-point sermon has fallen on hard times, probably because preachers who thought there should be three points pushed and shoved material into a three-point format when there weren't three points at all. It was too often a predictable, artificial and unsuitable pattern. A three-point sermon is also artificial where the sermon takes on a narrative form, as a plot unfolding. Yet there are times where a three-point sermon is perfectly suited to convey the message.

After deciding on your main point, if you find yourself wanting to say two, three or four things about it, let the sermon fall into that pattern. Tell the congregation you have "three things to say about this text/message/theme," and make sure they understand what they are in the flow of the sermon. Even more importantly make sure the audience never gets lost in just one of the points, but always knows that each of the points is related to the center.

The symbol for the classic "three-point sermon" — Introduction, One, Two, Three, Conclusion — is the bicycle wheel with two, three, four spokes radiating from the main point at the center. There's nothing magical about the number three. A two-point sermon can be just as good, or even four-point, if it's done clearly.

This type of sermon has an obvious strength: One can say various things *about* the theme, and if the preacher makes clear what the main theme is and how each point is related to it, the sermon can cover a lot of ground and still hang together coherently. It is especially suitable for epistle texts, which often do include several thoughts in just a verse or two.

57

One of England's greatest preachers, Charles Haddon Spurgeon, whose ministry in London spanned almost the entire last half of the 1800s, once preached a New Year's sermon on 1 Peter 5:10, "But the God of all grace, who has called us unto his eternal glory by Christ Jesus ... make you perfect, establish, strengthen and settle you." He chose as the central theme of the sermon and its title, "A New Year's Benediction," and the text itself gave him a four-point sermon: Perfection, Establishment, Strengthening and Settling.³⁴

James Stewart, one of Scotland's greatest preachers in this century, preached a sermon on Hebrews 12:22-25, "But you have come to Mount Zion ... and to the assembly of the first-born ..." Rich descriptions of the communion of saints tumble out one after the other in this short text. Rev. Stewart titled his sermon "Why Go To Church?" and organized the thoughts of the text into five points. Notice how clearly the structure is outlined in these excerpts:

> *It is an amazing wealth of suggestion that this writer has piled up here in disorderly profusion. Can we get some order out of it? I think we can. He is saying five things about our fellowship of Christian worship in the church.*
>
> *He begins with: it is a spiritual fellowship. . . . we can doubt the spiritual realities no longer, and we know we are going to be restless until we rest in God. God grants that this may happen every time we come up into his courts . . .*
>
> *I pass to the second fact our text underlines concerning the fellowship of Christian worship: it is a universal fellowship . . . . It is an incomparable thing, this universal fellowship. And every time you come to church, says this writer to the Hebrews, this is the fellowship you enter . . .*
>
> *I pass to the third description he gives of our fellowship in Christian worship. It is an immortal fellowship . . . . "You are come to the spirits of just men made perfect" — the immortal fellowship . . .*

Fourth, it is a divine fellowship ... and every time you come to worship, says this writer to the Hebrews, you can be quite certain you are coming to Jesus ...

One other fact about our fellowship in worship he adds, and so makes an end: it is a redeeming fellowship .... Where should any of us be if that were not true, if Christianity were not above everything else a religion of redemption?[35]

Keeping It Clear

A two/three/four-point sermon is a risky form for two reasons.

First, if the structure is not made clear, the sermon becomes a cluttered, gloppy muddle. If Stewart had not divided his thoughts into five clearly defined categories in the above sermon, it would have been a rambling, meandering jumble of thoughts about going to church.

No doubt you have listened to a sermon where the pastor has announced his intention to say "three things" about the text. He states his first point, then several minutes later he says, "The third thing I'd like to say ...," and you're left wondering what the second point was. On one occasion I heard only the first two points of a three-point sermon, and not until I read it afterward did I see that near the end the preacher had begun a paragraph with "Finally ..." That began the third point. It was clear on paper, but nobody in the audience caught it. That's the problem: The preacher knew exactly what he was doing, but failed to make it clear to the audience.

The second risk with this format is the danger of having three or four mini-sermons with no unifying theme clear to the listener. This is a "scattered thoughts" kind of sermon which one often hears. A three-or-four-point sermon works when each point is about something, that is, clearly related to the main theme, and the congregation knows what the connection is. Spurgeon's sermon works, because the unifying idea is in the title and repeated throughout the sermon: the benediction of God. Stewart's sermon is unified by the title, "Why Go To Church?" and with the word "fellowship" which becomes a unifying theme.

The test of an effective two/three/four-point sermon is basic and simple:

Make sure the separate points are clearly stated and that the audience knows how they relate to the main theme.

There are various means of doing this.
- State your points briefly near the start of the sermon, then go over each one in the body of the sermon.
- Announce a point at the beginning, "The first point is ..." then summarize it very briefly at the end of that section, leading into the next point: "That's the first thing I would say about the text. The second is ..."
- The conclusion of the sermon should be a brief summary, again making clear the structure of the sermon.

Some say that points should stand out so clearly that the speaker need not say one-two-three. That's true if people read sermons, since a reader can look back and review the points. But for an audience who will hear it only once, a good speaker makes the structure crystal clear. The listener who got it anyway won't mind, and the listener whose attention wandered will appreciate it!

I have done an exercise with pastors which illustrates how essential such clarity is. Years ago my father preached a sermon on Thomas (2 Easter, John 20:19-31).[36] His title was, "Where Will You Station Yourself?" Thomas did not see the risen Christ because he was not with the other disciples when Jesus appeared to them. The main point of the sermon was that there are places where God meets people, and that we can rely on encountering God in those places if we station ourselves there. The word "station" was the controlling image, or red thread, throughout the sermon, in the title, mentioned in the sermon itself and in the concluding sentence.

The body of the sermon fell naturally into three points, listing those places where we will meet God: 1) in word and sacrament; 2) within the fellowship of believers, his church; 3) in the company of the world's needy. Those three points are not only diverse, but each is a huge theme in itself.

The sermon worked because each of the points was related to the theme stated in the title and in the sermon: Where will we station ourselves? When people went home and thought about the sermon, the first thing they might recall would be the words in the title which they saw in the bulletin, "station yourself." From there they could easily reconstruct the sermon in their minds around the three points.

I retyped the sermon, but took away its coherence. I removed the unifying words — station/stationed — and eliminated any mention of three points. Then I gave the sermon a bland and unimaginative title, "Thomas Sees and Believes." I left each paragraph as it was, but rearranged them into a stream-of-consciousness sort of flow about Thomas — Jesus — Word — Bible — church — sacraments — the world's needy people.

Each paragraph was wonderfully written. The language was rich and colorful. But the sermon was a sprawling, meandering mess. A listener might be enthralled by the language, but by the final hymn she would have forgotten any point at all.

I had removed only a few words, but those few words gave structure to the sermon. They had informed the audience what the central theme was and what was said about it. They were small changes, but they made a world of difference.

Whatever form the sermon takes, the question for the preacher is: Is the message made clear to the listener?

Chapter 5
Structure And Movement

*"Why should I listen? I've heard so many of his sermons
I know what he's going to say anyway."*
— An usher who regularly "ducked out"
for a cup of coffee during the sermon.

What keeps people listening to a sermon? One basic answer is: curiosity about how it will end. Once the sermon becomes predictable, people's attention drifts off.

A good sermon must have flow or movement. A film, television program or story grabs our attention early on, and we are caught up in wanting to know how it comes out. Narrative preaching appeals to people not only because it is based on stories from life itself, but we listen to stories to see how they end. One can build in this same kind of movement into a sermon and keep the audience's attention.

The "Movement" Of The Sermon

A sermon is made up of different components, pieces, or chunks. To hold the audience's attention, these pieces have to be arranged so that they unfold with a sense of movement or dynamics. Charles L. Bartow, who taught speech and homiletics at Princeton Theological Seminary, urges preachers to listen to their own sermons for such a movement:

> *Principle number one for the listening preacher: Attend to the movement of thought in preaching and be prepared to move with it, for preaching that is true preaching will never let you rest content with some static arrangement of ideas.*[37]

63

David Buttrick suggests we look at our sermons as a series of "moves," as a developing narrative. "Preaching involves plotting," he says, and "plot is all-important."[38] Eugene Lowry, Professor of Preaching and Communication at the St. Paul School of Theology in Kansas City, is convinced that "the term *plot* is key both to sermon preparation and to sermon presentation."[39]

After a few years of preaching I discovered that I had fallen into a pattern, where the chunks of my sermon were almost always arranged like this:

- Review of the text, its setting and message;
- Reflection of the human situation today;
- Comments on how the text addresses this situation, what the text says for us today;
- Some kind of illustration or story showing how this actually worked in somebody's life.

That's a good flow, but I realized how predictable I was becoming. Whenever a preacher becomes predictable, the audience tends to think, "Here he goes again; we've heard this before."

Curiosity keeps an audience's attention. The listener wonders where the pastor's going with this idea and how it will come out. Vary the format of your sermons. One obvious possibility was to reverse my usual flow, so the sermon looked like this:

- Telling a story or illustration.
- Making a connection from this story to show how it illustrates a circumstance about our lives.
- Returning to the text and making clear how it affects this particular circumstance from today's life.

One can use many other pieces — comparison with other Bible passages, a look at another episode in church history, a description of how life might be, and so on. Variety and change will keep people listening.

Tension

Interest is maintained by tension. With their shortened attention span, the attention of today's audience drifts off if they sense that you've made your point. That's why a sense of movement is so important. If listeners are wondering, "How's all this going to come out?" they lean forward on the edge of their seats and listen.

Academic, written prose tends to lose this sense of movement and tension. In composition class we are told to put the important elements of the sentence at the beginning, so that the eye can get the point immediately. Even in paragraph construction, the first sentence should be the theme sentence, so that the basic idea is stated first. One can read much faster that way, because one can read just the first sentences and skim the rest. Tension is eliminated in favor of immediate answers.

That style might be suited for the written communication of information, but it deadens an oral speech. Why listen any more if you've already got the point? In speaking, even when you have stated your point, you want the listener to wonder what you're going to say about it.

A sermon should be constructed to maintain tension. A good sermon contains a problem or a complication which the sermon is wrestling with. The dynamic of a sermon is to address that problem. Eugene Lowry calls it the "homiletical bind":

> *Likewise a sermon in its essential form is a premeditated plot which has as its key ingredient a sensed discrepancy, a homiletical bind.*[40]

Charles Bartow calls it the "fulcrum" or "crisis" point in the sermon.[41]

There are many ways to introduce this problem, complication, fulcrum, or crisis, such as the following statements:

- "No wonder the people around Jesus were surprised ..."
- "Do we really believe this in our age? ..."

65

- "At first glance these verses sound puzzling to us ..."
- "Consider how the values of our society oppose the Christian faith ..."
- "Maybe we would prefer if Jesus had never said this ..."

Such statements immediately jar the listeners, and they will listen carefully.

At a funeral for a middle-aged mother who left small children behind, the pastor used Psalm 121 as the text:

> *I lift up my eyes to the hills.*
> *From whence does my help come?*
> *My help comes from the Lord,*
> *   who made heaven and earth.*
> *He will not let your foot be moved,*
> *   he who keeps you will not slumber* ..
> *The Lord is your keeper; the Lord is your shade ...*

Rather than speaking generally about our confidence in eternal life than Jesus' resurrection — the true but predictable, "safe" theme — the pastor confronted head-on the feelings of the grievers:

> *As we think of Eleanor's last days and experience our own grief, it's hard not to ask the question: Lord, did you fall asleep? Lord, have you closed your eyes? Where was your shade as Eleanor endured the radiation therapy? Where is your shade as we are left exposed to the reality of Eleanor's absence? Lord, are you sleeping?*

No one's mind wandered as the pastor spoke aloud their own hidden pain and anger. They listened eagerly, waiting to hear how she would address the crisis in faith brought about by the young mother's death.

There are several ways of maintaining tension. You may have stated the main theme of your sermon at the beginning, then introduced the complication, followed by the resolution. The text itself may have suggested the problem, since the words and actions of Jesus usually produced the problem or

66

complication itself. The opposition of the world or difficulties in people's lives furnish plenty of problems.

Instead of stating the message of the sermon at the beginning, then developing it, one can lead up to the point of the sermon. Lowry describes such a form:

> *Like any good storyteller, the preacher's task is to "bring the folks home" — that is, resolve matters in the light of the gospel and in the presence of the people.*[42]

He proposes "five basic sequential stages to a typical sermonic process:"

> *1) upsetting the equilibrium,*
> *2) analyzing the discrepancy,*
> *3) disclosing the clue to resolution,*
> *4) experiencing the gospel, and*
> *5) anticipating the consequences.*[43]

Look For The Trouble

When we read a troublesome text, our first instinct is to shrink from the verses which cause trouble. For example, on a beautiful fall Sunday morning, the 21st Sunday after Pentecost, how can one possibly stand before a hard-working, middle-class congregation, all of whom are wealthy when measured on the scale of most of the world's population, and preach on the Cycle C Gospel, Mark 10:17-27, "It is easier for a camel to go through the eye of a needle than for a rich man to enter the kingdom of God"?

I heard a sermon on that text, where the pastor had clearly thrown up his arms in surrender. He skipped to the last verse, "With humans it is impossible, but ... all things are possible with God," and sought immediate refuge in the heart of his faith, justification by grace: "On the basis of our own works we would be judged and condemned, but we look for salvation to the grace of God in Jesus Christ." It was a satisfactory exposition on the doctrine of justification, but it avoided the point of the text. We cannot read that text without confronting and struggling with the question of wealth.

When the people in the congregation heard the text being read, no doubt the words of Jesus jolted them, as they were forced to ask themselves if their possessions were stumbling blocks in God's kingdom. They sat down, wondering what the preacher would say about these troublesome verses, but they left the church empty when he steered clear around them.

If a reading causes trouble when you read it, it will no doubt do the same for many of your hearers on Sunday morning. You have the listeners' attention from the beginning. Plunge right into the trouble and you keep their attention.

Of course it is easier to avoid the trouble. If you have not given yourself time for preparation, you will sit at your desk Saturday night still wondering what to say. At about 9:30 p.m. you will give up and preach on one of the other texts, losing the opportunity to guide the congregation through a tough passage. It takes time, prayer, study and reflection to get through the hard texts.

I remember working on Luke 6:17-26 (Epiphany 6), the Beatitudes in Luke. On first reading I was bothered that misery is praised ("Blessed are those who are poor ... hungry ... weep ... hated ... excluded ..."), while those who are satisfied are condemned ("Woe to you who are rich ... full ... laugh ... spoken well of ..."). Our first impression is that only those who suffer can be Christians. What other reading could there be? The text would level a severe judgment on my listeners, with no relief in sight.

As I worked with this text the direction for my sermon came from two insights:

- The context of the passage: This is early in Jesus' ministry; he has just called his disciples (vv. 12-16) and now begins to tell them what discipleship might mean for them.

- The phrase buried at the end of verse 22: "... on account of the Son of man!" This phrase is behind each of the "beatitude" verses as well as the "woe" verses.

68

That put the whole text in a different light. The primary issue is not whether one is poor or rich, weeping or happy, but whether we are followers of Jesus. The issue is discipleship. The circumstances of our lives are the by-product of our following Jesus. "On account of the Son of man" is the leitmotif of the whole section. "On account of Jesus" we might be poor, unhappy, reviled. If that's what discipleship causes, we can still rejoice that the kingdom is ours. The joy of being a disciple enables us to rise above those other circumstances. Suffering is not whitewashed or minimized, but there is another dimension to the Christian life: We are part of the kingdom through it all. Conversely, woe to those who have everything, but are not part of the kingdom.

The sermon's message was broadened beyond the narrow confines of a superficial first reading. But it took time, prayer and study to come to this deeper meaning of the text.

Sometimes the clash of a text with everyday life helps you through the trouble. Preaching on the Friday after Easter 2, I determined to follow the daily lectionary and was drawn to the Old Testament text for the day, Daniel 3:1-18, the account of the three Hebrew men being thrown into the fiery furnace. Two problems were obvious:

(1) Many people face trials in their lives, even suffering for their faith, and are not rescued from the fiery furnaces. (The congregation had just observed Yom Ha-Shoah, the Day of the Holocaust a few days before, and I wondered how today's Jews read this passage!)

(2) The reading for that day was the first part of the story and did not include the rescue from the fiery furnace. Can one preach on half a story? The lectionary would finish the story the next day, but I was preaching just the first day of the reading.

People listening to the text would wonder: Do such miraculous rescues take place today, and how can one read only the first half of the story?

The solution to the problem and the point of the sermon came from the text itself. After hearing the mighty king

69

Nebuchadnezzar's ultimatum to worship heathen gods or die, Shadrach, Meshach and Abednago responded that they would not capitulate. "If it be so," they said, "our God whom we serve is able to deliver us from the burning fiery furnace." The reading for that day ended with verse 18, as the three young men continue:

> *"But if not, be it known to you, O king, that we will not serve your gods or worship the golden image which you have set up."*

The theme of the sermon jumped out with those first three words: "But, if not . . ." Those gallant Hebrew youth believed that God could rescue them, "but if not," even if God did not do so, they would stand firm. Faith does not venture forth with guarantees of success, but it marches out in trust that come what may, God will see us through even the jaws of death. Martin Luther went to Worms in 1521 knowing the chances of being burned as a heretic were fairly high. He survived the fiery furnace. Jan Hus traveled to Konstanz a century earlier and was burned at the stake for his faith. The endings of the two stories were different, but it was the same faith which carried both men forward.

The sermon didn't need the rest of the story. The text ended with the unshakable faith of verses 17, 18: We know that God can rescue us, "but if not" we stand firm nonetheless!

Working through a troublesome text takes time, prayer and reflection. But it can open up new insights and lift your preaching out of worn-out ruts into new and adventuresome paths. It will also enrich the listeners, because they too have wondered about these difficult texts!

Remember The Skeptics

When I first started teaching homiletics, I told the students always to preach with two assumptions in mind:

(1) Assume the congregation is half asleep. It may not actually be true, but the assumption will make us better preachers.

(2) Whatever interesting points you make from the text, always assume some people need to hear the basic, central gospel of God's love and mercy in Jesus Christ. We deal with many issues in the course of a church year and give many interesting examples, but the gospel must always be at the center. There are people in every congregation whose souls are in agony, and they need to hear the gospel of sin and grace this Sunday.

When I told my predecessor, Arndt Halvorson, about these two assumptions, he suggested adding a third:

(3) Assume there are skeptics in the audience. Remember those who are wondering if it's all true. This assumption will push you to avoid easy cliches and deal head-on with people's doubts and problems.

For example, you are preparing for All Saints' Sunday. You are planning on concentrating on the text from Revelation, the glorious vision of the saints in heaven. Your main point will be that this vision of saints together in God's kingdom sustained the early Christians under persecution as well as us today. The sermon could easily become a pollyannaish description of how good it is to be part of a parish family with the hope of heaven before us, and so on.

Now think of the skeptics. There are some in the audience who have experienced pain from fellow Christians. There may be some who are desperately lonely and nobody in the congregation has given them a second glance. There will be those who think about the scandal of TV preachers and wonder if Christians are all hypocrites. Some may experience far more support from their bowling league than from fellow Christians.

Suddenly you're forced to think about people who are skeptical of the Revelation vision. Cliches won't work anymore. The sermon must plunge into these hard questions.

You discover the resources already there in the scriptures, where saints are portrayed realistically as people who do fall short of God's ideals. You see the Revelation vision as a group of imperfect people who have been made part of the body of Christ and who are all sustained by the guiding Spirit of God. The church is not a country club for successful people, but a hospital for sinners, all under the care of the great Physician. With the skeptics in mind, your sermon takes on a whole new perspective, one which sees Christians with stark realism, yet with the promises of grace entering powerfully into the human situation. The skeptic can say, "Yes, that's what we're like all right, but thank God he's brought us together!"

"Flow" Sermon

In my experience, sermons do not usually fall into a three-point format, and it violates the sense of the text if one tries to chop a sermon into "points." More often the sermon takes on a "flow," from one piece to the other. Rather than a bicycle-wheel, with separate points radiating like spokes from a central hub, the sermon is more like a string of beads, one piece after the other. After selecting a main theme, I decided on the "flow" or "movement" to drive the main theme home. The task is to put the elements together so they flow well from start to finish. Then we are back to "arranging the pieces," discussed above. Most important is to keep the format flexible, let the sense and drama of the text shape the sermon.

Opening Paragraph

With the short attention span of today's audience, the first sentence and first paragraph are especially important. If they don't grab people's attention, the whole sermon may never get off the ground. A good beginning does two things:
(1) catches the people's attention;
(2) leads into the theme of the sermon.
It captures attention in different ways. It may plunge into the text with some creative thinking or provocative questions. Or it might paint a picture which fires the imagination. It may

be a story which strikes the audience and starts them thinking. Another possibility is to use the introduction to heighten the sense of expectation or tension in the sermon.

A good introduction not only leads into the theme of the sermon, but actually becomes the theme of the sermon. A vivid introduction which leads to, or illustrates, a side issue of the text may actually detract from the main point of the sermon. The introduction must lead to the main theme of the sermon for it to be effective.

For example, I heard a sermon for the Fourth Sunday in Lent, Cycle C, the Parable of the Prodigal Son, Luke 15:1-3, 11-32. The preacher began something like this:

> *Many of us can look back on our life and see wasted years. I'm embarrassed to remember how I loafed through high school and college. I got poor grades in high school and then when I moved to a college dorm I spent most of my time watching TV with a beer can in my hand. I barely made it through college, and even then I hardly knew what to do with my life. I got a job, but it wasn't what I really wanted to do ...*

The introduction rambled on a while longer, leading us through a few more aimless years, including mention of a friend whose straying life led tragically to his suicide. Finally came the transition to the text:

> *The young man in our text wasted part of his life too ...*

The problem is that the theme of the introduction — wasting the years of one's youth — dominated the sermon, far overshadowing the real message of the text, namely the father's loving acceptance of his returning son. Listeners thinking about the sermon later will remember the wasted years of the youth and the tragic death of the other young man, rather than the father.

A good introduction may also accomplish a third purpose:
   (3) provides an image which carries throughout the rest of the sermon.

73

This third purpose is particularly helpful, because the introduction itself contains the "red thread" which holds the sermon together for the audience.

Scottish-born Peter Marshall, pastor of New York Avenue Presbyterian Church in Washington, D.C., during the years of World War II, was preparing a sermon about Abraham. His texts were Genesis 12:1-3, the call of Abraham, and Hebrews 11:8, "By faith Abraham ... went out, not knowing whither he went." He needed an introduction to describe what it must have been like to venture forth in faith when one doesn't know one's destination or fate. This is how he began his sermon:

> *I do not know what picture the phrase "under sealed orders" suggests to you — to me it recalls very vividly a scene from the first world war, when I was a little boy spending vacations at the Scottish seaport.*
>
> *I saw a gray destroyer slipping hurriedly from port in response to some urgent commands ... I watched the crew hurry their preparations for sailing, watched them cast off the mooring hawsers ... saw the sleek ship get under way, as she rose to meet the lazy swell of a summer evening ... Her Morse lamp was winking on the control bridge aft, and I watched her until she was lost in the mists of the North Sea.*
>
> *She was a mystery vessel. She had sailed under orders. Not even her officers knew her destination or the point of rendezvous. We all start in life, going — we know not where. It will be revealed later. But meanwhile we must go out in faith — under sealed orders.*[44]

The picture of the destroyer leaving port rivets one's attention on what is to come. Your mind sees the gray ship disappearing into the fog, and the tension of a mysterious war-time mission captures you for the remainder of the sermon.

74

But this image not only introduced the theme of the sermon; it became the theme of the sermon. Rev. Marshall reinforced the image by using the phrase of the opening sentence as the title of the sermon, "Under Sealed Orders." The sermon concluded by returning to this opening image and fixing it in our minds:

> *We are living in a hazardous epoch of history ... You are leaving port under sealed orders and in a troubled period. You cannot know whither you are going or what you are to do. But why not take a Pilot on board who knows the nature of your sealed orders from the outset, and who will shape your entire voyage accordingly? He knows the shoals and the sandbanks, the rocks and the reefs. He will steer you safely into that celestial harbor where your anchor will be cast for eternity. Let his mighty nail-pierced hands hold the wheel, and you will be safe.*
>
> *Now is a splendid time to entrust your life to him, now, as you begin. Give him your life. He will treasure it, even as [he treasures] you.*
>
> *Then, though you may not know what will be your harbor, you will know your Pilot ... And all will be well.* [45]

If somebody who heard that sermon was asked later that day, "What was the sermon about?" he would not likely say, "I really don't know what he was getting at!" He might not immediately remember the text. His first memory might not be Abraham, the actual theme of the text, nor the meaning of Abraham for our time, that we too venture forth in faith.

The first image which would come to mind for the listener would be the gray destroyer gliding into the icy mists of the North Sea. From there the listener would recall the rest of the sermon in his mind — Abraham, the text and the application of the text to us. The introduction fixed an image which became the controlling image of the whole sermon.

Carrying the introduction throughout the sermon and the conclusion doesn't always work. Nor would you want every sermon to fall into that same pattern. But when it works, it gives the sermon a unity of structure which cannot help but convey the message to the audience.

Titles

Titles can reinforce the message of the sermon. It is the first thing about the sermon the listeners actually see — in the bulletin, the sign board outside, or in the newspapers. An effective title can:
- provoke curiosity about the sermon;
- pose a question to stimulate thinking; or
- lead into the theme of the sermon.

Preaching on Matthew 17:19, "Why could not we cast him out?" Martin Luther King, Jr. titled the sermon "The Answer to a Perplexing Question." If the people paid attention to the gospel being read, they would have heard the question posed in the text and known the sermon would deal with it. Rev. King began the sermon by restating the question of the text:

> *But the problem that has always hampered man has been his inability to conquer evil by his own power. In pathetic amazement, he asks, "Why can I not cast it out? Why can I not remove this evil from my life?"*[46]

He went on to give two false ways to eliminate evil: either by our attempt to remove evil through our own power, or by waiting passively for God to solve the problem. Then he restarted the question of the text on our level:

> *What, then, is the answer to life's perplexing question, "How can evil be cast out of our individual and collective lives?" If the world is not to be purified by God alone nor by man alone, who will do it?*[47]

76

He moved to the answer, responding to the two false answers given earlier:

> *The answer is found in an idea which is distinctly different from the two we have discussed, for neither God nor man will individually bring the world's salvation. Rather, both man and God, made in a marvelous unity of purpose through an overflowing love as the free gift of himself . . .* [48]

The theme of the title has become the theme of the sermon, and it is concluded in the final paragraph:

> *Herein we find the answer to a perplexing question. Evil can be cast out, not by man alone nor by a dictatorial God who invades our lives, but when we open the door and invite God through Christ to enter . . .* [49]

It all fit together. The structure of the sermon was made very clear from the start, and words "perplexing question" became the unifying idea, from the title through the concluding paragraph. The audience's attention was maintained as we were kept waiting for the answer posed by the text. The title was clear from the start and was used throughout the sermon.

One can also use a title to heighten expectation and tension. People will listen carefully, because they wonder, "What does the title have to do with all this?"

Fred Craddock preached a sermon on Galatians 1:11-24, the transformation from Saul the persecutor to Paul, the apostle to the Gentiles. He noted how difficult it must have been for the early Jewish Christians to accept Gentiles as Christians, and pointed out how our own prejudices can become barriers to our discipleship. [50]

An obvious title would have been "Overcoming Prejudices," an accurate but banal description of the sermon's theme. Such a title wouldn't spark anybody's interest.

Instead, Craddock's imaginative title "Praying Through Clenched Teeth" piques our curiosity, helps us to imagine how Paul must have felt when God first called him to preach to the Gentiles, and leads us to wonder how often we ourselves pray unwillingly. The title grabs our attention and embodies the content of the sermon.

In crafting a sermon, knowing how people's minds wander, take steps to seize and hold their interest!

Chapter 6
Creative Preaching

I would urge every preacher to attempt an experimental sermon occasionally, especially if he or she is normally a very routine, conventional person.[51]

— John Killinger

Change attracts attention. Every preacher knows this after watching people's attention shift to a child walking up the aisle and out the door to the bathroom. I was in a church once where a bird was flying around the sanctuary. The pastor could just as well have been reading out of the phone book for all the attention the sermon retained.

A change in sermon style also attracts the attention of the congregation. Preaching the same way every Sunday to today's audience deadens your preaching. Varying your usual style and doing something different in the pulpit on occasion will not only broaden your own skills and outlook, but it will reawaken interest among the listeners.

The last chapter proposed varying one's flow, organizing the material to keep the listener's attention. This chapter suggests using a different kind of sermon now and then.

New Forms

There is no one correct style of preaching. The gospel is constant, but styles and forms can change. Over the years no other group in history has used more variety in communication than Christian preachers. The Christian church has been

79

in the forefront of new communication forms — from the sermons and letters of Paul, the four gospels, the dauntless missionary monks of medieval Europe, the mystery dramas performing Bible stories all over Europe, the stained glass artists and sculptors who portrayed the gospel through their art, musicians who wrote music for the church, the courageous preachers of the Reformation era, the frontier tent preachers of this country, and the missionaries who have fanned out around the world. The new age of printing was inaugurated with, what else? the Bible.

Yet today we Christian preachers seem to be oblivious to the new world of communication. Advertisers, politicians and entertainers have taken the pulse of the new audience and adapted their style. Can it be that for the first time in history the church is not taking its message seriously enough to vary its communication style?

There is a reason for this reluctance. We are suspicious of passing fads or gimmickry in preaching. The gospel is too precious for that. Many of us avoid new forms of preaching because they draw attention to the style of the sermon, away from the text, or they may be irresponsible to the text. People might go home raving about a chancel drama the pastor did with four other people acting out their parts, instead of a regular sermon. Yet if they can't remember what the message was, the gospel was not served.

There is a wide variety one can use in verbal communication which will convey the gospel. Variety in preaching can reawaken a congregation which has grown accustomed to the same sermon format every Sunday. Preaching which has fallen into a groove may really be in a rut.

The gospel can be conveyed in many ways, and a good preacher should consider nontraditional ways of communicating. If the message of the text can be conveyed more effectively with a different kind of sermon, try it. A nontraditional sermon even once or twice a year will make a huge difference in how your congregation looks forward to preaching.[52]

Telling The Story

One source for a new style of preaching is the Bible itself.

Recruiting Sunday school teachers, every pastor has heard the excuse, "I don't know enough about the Bible to teach Sunday school." For some this might be false modesty, but the fact is that more and more people don't know much about the Bible these days! We live in an age of increasing and alarming ignorance about the Bible.

The best Bible teaching time in a congregation is the sermon. Offer a Bible study class and 10-20 people will come, probably the same persons who attended the last Bible study class. Far more people listen to the Sunday morning sermon.

Preaching should tell the story, and that means the stories in the Bible. The biblical text should be the engine that drives the sermon. Unfortunately in many sermons the text is the diving board into the sermon. The pastor uses the text to jump into the theme of the sermon, then swims around in the theme and never comes back to the text. The text becomes a pretext for the sermon.

A truly biblical sermon can take various forms:

- **thematic,** where the theme comes from and is tightly bound to the text;
- **expository,** where the preacher goes through the text verse by verse;
- **illustrative,** where illustrations and stories are used to convey the story or narrative of the text;
- **retelling,** where a large part of the sermon is the text itself, retold in the preacher's words.

Old Testament and gospel texts which are stories in themselves lend themselves to retelling. Listeners often pay little attention to texts as they are being read during the service, but will listen carefully when preachers retell the story in their own words as part of the sermon. If we truly believe in the power of the Word, we can confidently let the Bible speak for itself!

Black preachers are masters at this. The black church in this country grew among mostly illiterate people. The sermon was for them what stained-glass and sculpture were for the medieval church — means of teaching the Bible stories to people who couldn't read.

A black pastor told me, "The first requirement for preaching in a black congregation is to be able to tell a Bible story." A good black preacher will retell the story with such color and drama that it comes alive in your mind. His advice to me was, "Dress it up some ... but don't mess with it!"

"Dress it up some ..." A good storyteller adds details to the story to help the listener see it better. One describes people and recreates conversations that are not actually in the biblical text.

In 1943 Peter Marshall preached to a Good Friday congregation in Detroit.[53] His title was "Were You There?" and most of the sermon was a retelling of the *via dolorosa,* Jesus' agonizing journey through the streets of Jerusalem carrying the cross to his crucifixion on the Golgotha hill. The sermon described the noises of the crowds, the glint of sunlight on the Roman soldiers' armor, their hardbitten cruelty as they pushed the crowds back to make way for Jesus, the anguish among Jesus' friends as they watched the procession, the thud of the hammer as the nails were driven into hands and feet, and finally the excruciating agony Jesus suffered as he hung there.

The listener saw the Passion of Jesus in the mind's eye. With the story vivid in our minds, Rev. Marshall moved to the conclusion: "Were you there?" Yes, the listener was there, because the story had come alive in our minds.

"... but don't mess with it!" my black friend continued. "My people know all these stories. If I add something that doesn't belong there, or get something wrong, they know, they know right away, and they let me know!"

In retelling the story, the preacher dresses it up, but doesn't add things that don't belong. One has to be creative without altering or violating the message of the text. The details have to be consistent and credible with the story. They must not distract from it or shift its meaning. The preacher has to know the historical setting well enough to keep the descriptions accurate.

We preachers do this consistently even without thinking. For instance, preaching on the story of the Prodigal Son, one might say,

On the day that his boy left him, the joy went out of the father's life. As he watched his spirited and splendid son walk away, memories flooded his mind — the joy of the boy's birth, the games they had played, the excitement of the boy when they had gone fishing, all the times they had worked side-by-side in the fields. Finally his son disappeared down the road, and with tear-stained cheeks he turned and went back home, to a house that now seemed lonely and empty.

Most of those words and descriptions are not in the text, but they are consistent with the situation, and the story comes alive to those who listen. Every parent in the congregation whose child has grown up and left home, even in happy circumstances, will identify with the story and, more importantly, realize in a new light the meaning of the story as it unfolds. Being struck afresh by the father's deep love for his son, the listener realizes how profoundly God loves his wayward children on earth.

When the story is retold well, people will catch glimpses of things they never heard before, even in the most familiar of stories. Old stories become new again. Unexpected insights flood the mind.

This is not an easy kind of sermon to preach. It takes creativity to retell the story well, and some people do it better than others. One must also learn about the background and historical context of the text, so that the details of the story do not contradict the setting. Retelling the story well takes effort, but it is well worth it to make the Bible come alive.

Visual Aids

Most traditional preachers shy away from visual aids because they can so easily be trite or corny. For a visual generation, however, they can also be very effective. They give the listener a "hook" by which the message of the sermon sticks to them.

For example, I preached a post-Easter sermon on 1 Peter 2:9-10:

> *But you are a chosen race, a royal priesthood, a holy nation, God's own people, that you may declare the wonderful deeds of him who called you out of darkness into his marvelous light. Once you were no people, but now you are God's people ... (1 Peter 2:4-10)*

The title of the sermon was "How Do You Identify Yourself?" The theme was that we are more than human beings here on this earth. When we introduce ourselves we give our name, address, then add items such as our profession, our family situation, hobbies, and so on. Yet from the larger perspective of all eternity, we should introduce ourselves first as a baptized child of God.

To make the point I held up my passport. When we lived in Europe, I said, we spoke the language of the land, paid taxes, and our children attended the local schools. But my residence there was only temporary. My true citizenship was elsewhere. I was a citizen of the United States, and wherever I traveled, my passport was the sign of my true identity. Baptism is our passport to God's people. No matter where we are or what we do, we Christians belong to a greater kingdom, and that is our true identity. Many listeners still remember the passport sermon, and remembering the passport, they recall the message of the text.

Another time I preached a sermon titled "Precious in the Sight of God." The point of the sermon was that human beings are precious not because of any inherent quality within us, but because we are created by God, who has loved us enough to send his Son to die for our reconciliation and salvation. We are precious because we are precious to God.

84

I needed an object which had value not in itself but given to it. First I held up a piece of high-quality carpet about a foot square. It was high-priced carpet, superbly made from fine wool. Then I held up a piece of brand new bond stationery paper. Both items had value in themselves.

Next I held up a $20 bill. It was old and crumpled, so the paper wasn't worth anything. Since it was all covered with letters, numbers and designs, one couldn't even use it for note paper. By itself it was worth nothing.

Yet it was by far the most valuable of the three items. Why? Because a higher power said it was. It was valuable because the United States government said it was, simple as that. In a similar way we human beings are precious because the Almighty Creator of this whole vast universe loves us and has named us his children.

The possibilities of visual aids are limitless, and no doubt every reader has used them. They can also distract from the sermon. If the connection between the object and the sermon theme is obscure or contrived, people might recall the object but not the message. If the object illustrates something other than the main point of the sermon, the message is obscured.

One pastor did a series of first person sermons, speaking as a biblical character. For each one he used an object to help the congregation recognize the character — sunglasses for the blind man (John 9), a plaster death mask for Lazarus (John 11), a jar and towel for the woman who washed Jesus' feet (Luke 7), and so on. The sermons were preached some time ago, but listeners still remember them, because they recall the objects used.

More Than One Preacher

There are several kinds of sermons where the pastor is joined by other persons — dialogue sermons, sermons as conversations between two or more persons, participation from members of the audience, and so on. They take a great deal of time in preparation, but they can be powerful means of proclamation if done well.

A change in preaching style is particularly effective on those occasions where we repeat the same texts year after year. The preacher often wonders, "What shall I say this year?"

On a Reformation Sunday, Wisconsin pastor Gordon Thorpe did something different. People came into the sanctuary and noticed a door placed in the front of the church. The pastor began the sermon speaking in the first-person as Martin Luther, recreating the historical setting of that first Reformation Day, when the reformer posted his 95 Theses to challenge the sale and traffic in indulgences. He spoke about Luther's appearance at the Congress at Worms in 1521, where before the assembled rulers of the Empire he courageously defended his convictions. Then he asked,

> *"Are there Lutherans today who know what they believe and whose beliefs are really important? . . . Is there anyone here today who thinks that . . ."*

At that moment a scientist in the congregation came forward and said,

> *". . . this belief that God is our creator has affected my life and my work in many ways. As a caretaker of God's creation I'm careful that the actions and the decisions that I take as a computer engineer do not destroy this universe that belongs to God, but rather preserve it."*

He said that God's creative power is at work not only in the creation, but also in the lives of himself and the people in the church.

No sooner had he finished than another person came forward and said,

> *"I'd like to share my convictions with you this morning . . . I strongly believe that Jesus Christ has guided me through many trying and sometimes dangerous situations."*

She called upon the people in the congregation to respond to Christ's love by reaching out in love to others.

A high school teacher stood up and told how

> "... when I was an infant my parents brought me to church, not for a symbolic ceremony but for a real miracle at the altar in which I was touched in baptism by Jesus. It was also important as I got to an adult stage when I could make decisions for myself and choose my own way. I asked God to guide my life, to be part of my life, to help me daily and to lead me ... I will always sin and I will always need to confess it, and I will always be forgiven for as long as I do so ..."

The last to come forward was a college instructor, who told of his trust in God's constant presence at various times of his life. He testified to his faith "that Jesus Christ will never leave me nor forsake me. On Christ the solid rock I stand."

As the speakers finished, they took their statements and nailed them to the door, just as Luther had posted his 95 Theses on the Castle Church door in Wittenberg.

The pastor closed the sermon by inviting members of the congregation to write their own statements of faith on blank bulletin inserts and nail them to the door. The sermon was followed by several hymns, and the singing was punctuated by the sound of hammer blows as people came forward. The message of the day was the message of Reformation Day, but because the style was different, it will be long remembered by people who were there.

Drama

One Good Friday our youth group performed *Construction,* a play designed for a church chancel by Ralph Stone. The play begins as nine people walk down the aisle and assemble at the front of the church, wondering where they are and what they're supposed to do there. Representing various kinds of persons, they notice a lot of construction materials laying around and decide they should build something. But what? After much bickering and arguing they decide they should build a wall to protect themselves from anybody who might be out there, although it has become clear to the audience that these people haven't learned to live with themselves, say nothing of learning to live with anybody in other areas.

As the second act begins there is a large piece of cardboard across the chancel, painted to look like a stone wall. A stranger comes down the aisle and claims to have the blueprint for what the designer really had in mind for the construction materials. Much to their surprise he tells them:

> *"A bridge ... Not a wall, not a wall at all. We have far too many of them as it is. We need more bridges — bridges over which the traffic can flow both ways, bridges that take you from here to other places and bring other places to you here."*[4]

The people are shocked, since they have grown secure and protective with their wall. The dispute builds until everyone grabs tools and attacks the Builder. At the moment they put him to death, the lights in the church go out, leaving only one spotlight on the cross at the front of the church — the crucified Builder whose blueprints from the Designer were rejected by his own people.

The message of the play conveyed the message of the cross in a new and thought-provoking way. Even more importantly, in the process of preparing and rehearsing the play the youth understood in a deeper way what Jesus' crucifixion really meant.

I could have preached a sermon on that same theme, even telling the story of the play itself. However, seeing it enacted on the stage was a far more powerful way of communicating the message.

The Word In Other Forms

I recently heard a highly effective sermon given as a letter. Speaking in the first person, the preacher explained that he was a Jew, still living in Babylon, descended from the Jews who had been exiled to Babylon 500 years before Jesus was born. He had received a letter from a scholarly friend of his, who had seen in the stars a message that a king was born to the Jews in Palestine and who had gone to find him. He then unfolded a scroll and read the letter from one of the wise men, describing the Christmas story and the search to find the baby from his perspective. It was done with creativity and imagination, enabling us listeners to experience the story from a new perspective, with the sense of awe and wonder which those magi must have felt. The familiar Christmas story came alive in a new way.

The sermon had taken much thorough preparation, because the preacher had done research on the Jewish diaspora group in Babylon, the study of ancient astronomy and the story of magi. The sermon never violated the flow or the content of the biblical story but was consistent with what we know about the historical details of that era.

Throughout the church's history music has been a vehicle for the gospel. Particularly among young people, some of the most effective Christian communication is being done through music. This can also be done in sermons. I have heard preachers quote or sing hymns, have the choir or congregation sing a hymn verse, have somebody else play or sing, or play music on tape.

The power of music as a means of transmitting the gospel was made clear to me on a recent trip to Germany. A Christian who had lived through the harsh years of communist rule in East Germany told me,

"The Marxist government opposed modern music such as jazz and rock-and-roll as evil influences from the West. Yet they let us sing the wonderful music of the

89

church, such as Bach's cantatas, his St. Matthew's Passion and the Christmas Oratorio. God's Word was heard through the music by many people who would not have been in church, and that Word took root in people's hearts!"

Imaginative preaching can use music, and of course the gospel is being communicated by music throughout the whole worship service.

The gospel can also be communicated through stories from literature. One congregation in North Dakota will never forget Henry Van Dyke's *The Other Wise Man,* because it was told in a creative fashion one Christmas. Just as the pastor began to preach the phone rang. An usher handed a note to the pastor, who said, "I have to leave for a few minutes." He motioned to a member of the congregation and said, "You know some good Christmas stories. Tell one until I get back."

The speaker came forward and began telling Van Dyke's story, written a century ago. One of the wise men, Artaban, stopped to aid a dying man in the desert and thus missed the rendezvous with the others. To equip himself for the trip across the desert alone, he spent a sapphire, one of the gifts he had brought for the new-born king.

The speaker paused for a moment and said, "That's all of the story I can remember," and stepped down. Another person in the congregation got up and said, "I know what happens next," and told how the wise man arrived too late in Bethlehem, just as Herod's soldiers were sweeping in to kill the babies. She told how Artaban gave the captain of the band a beautiful ruby to protect a mother huddling in fear with her tiny child. It was another of his gifts, and for this gift of her child's life the mother blessed him with the benediction from the Old Testament.

The speaker sat down, and yet another got up. "There's more," she said, and continued the story. Just as she finished, the pastor returned and told how the story illustrates the message of Christmas. By then the congregation realized it had all been prepared beforehand, but probably no one who was there will forget that sermon.

Richard Jensen calls these kinds of creative ideas "stereo preaching," creative preaching which communicates to both the literal left side of the brain as well as the more intuitive right side.[55] Creative and nontraditional preaching done well on occasion can be enormously helpful to convey the gospel in fresh ways.

Chapter 7
Delivery

I once visited a church in which the minister delivered what seemed at the time to be an interesting sermon, but I couldn't quite grasp the real thrust of the message, because it was delivered in a monotone, most of it read with little warmth or enthusiasm. [The church secretary] agreed to mail me a copy of the sermon I'd just heard. When the sermon arrived in the mail and I read it, I realized that the structure of the message was coherent and sound and the points well made. I could hardly believe I was reading the same sermon I'd heard.[56]
— Homer K. Buerlein

Years ago the pastor was the best public speaker in town, perhaps the only one. The Sunday morning service may have been the best, or only, interesting event in town. Now the competition is fierce. A preacher is compared not with the pastor down the block, but with Dan Rather and Tom Brokaw, maybe even Arsenio Hall and Jay Leno. Even worse, people can stay home on Sunday morning and see a huge congregation, a gorgeous church with water fountains, a huge organ played by a virtuoso, a marvelous choir, probably singing with music memorized, and a pastor whose speaking skills rival those of the multi-million-dollar-salaried network stars.

Stiff competition! In addition there is probably a church not too far away which is imitating the "worship-as-entertainment" television style, and some people in your congregation are dropping hints that they like that style.

Effective Speaking

Thus far I have discussed how a sermon might be written with this new audience in mind. In the past, when the sermon manuscript lay completed on the desk, the pastor could sit back and say with satisfaction, "Finally, it's done!" All that remained was to read it to the congregation.

That's no longer true. With a completed manuscript we are half done. Now we have to learn it. A good sermon has to be well written and well delivered. In the age of television, many a fine sermon dies from poor delivery. Today we simply cannot be boring in the pulpit.

Communication is a learned skill. One isn't born with the ability to speak well; one works at it. There are basic and proven techniques for acquiring this skill, and with effort any preacher can improve.

The End Of Reading

For centuries the primary means of education has been teachers reading lectures. At some meetings the manuscript is distributed, and the speaker reads it while the audience follows along on the printed page. The delivery can be pedantic, because it's the printed page that's important.

Television has changed all that. It has returned us to an oral style, but with a twist.

In the early days of television broadcasters continued the universal style of reading to the audience. Remember when newscasters had papers in front of them and would look up and down?

Very soon they learned that the audience found that style distracting and impersonal. They realized instinctively that they had to return to direct, eye-to-eye communication to be effective. Fancy new teleprompting devices were developed, which restored the oral style of direct eye contact. The fact that they are still reading every word may be irrelevant.

Teleprompters create the illusion of direct speaking. You think they are looking right at you. Prompters are so sophisticated now that you cannot even notice the reporter's eyes moving.

The age of reading before an audience is gone! With the massive influence of television, teachers have discovered that the students are quickly bored by lectures read to them, no matter how good the material. Only in the upper levels of graduate school, where students have become re-accustomed to the educational world of print, do teachers read lectures, and even there an effective teacher leaves the script and speaks directly and personally to the students.

We have already noted that the impersonal nature of television has produced a passive audience. People are accustomed to being addressed directly, but they do not listen as well.

I know a preacher who writes excellent sermons. He reads them word-for-word, and he reads them very well, with expression, variety and energy in his voice. But the congregation's attention wanders, and when it is over many of them have not listened well at all. Why? Because they sense that the focus of his attention is on his paper. He looks up from time to time and scans his eyes over the audience because he knows that is good style, but the audience knows they are spectators to a performance. Not until I sat with a sick child in the nursery and heard his sermon over the loudspeaker — without seeing him at all — did I realize how well he preached. He might have been a fine radio preacher, but he was not effective in the pulpit with real people in front of him.

The result of our television mentality is that the preacher must capture and hold the audience's attention by speaking directly to them. Reading a sermon is the best way to kill it.

In my talks with laypersons one of the remarks I hear most often is, "The pastor just reads the sermon." There are a few rare people who can read a sermon and maintain direct audience contact, but no one should ever assume they are that type. No matter how good the content of a sermon is, if it's read it does not get across to today's audience.

In one adult forum a lady pleaded, "I wish the pastor would speak to us instead of reading!" One might wonder what the distinction is. The truth is that television has accustomed people to being spoken to, not read to. The manuscript has become a barrier between the speaker and audience. Unless your parish can afford $20,000 to install a teleprompter and a battery of technicians to operate it, you have to figure out some other way of freeing yourself from the manuscript. Television has changed our audience, and the reality is that we simply must get away from our scripts.

Working Free Of The Manuscript

Freeing oneself of the manuscript is one of the most difficult tasks for most pastors. Two things are true:

(1) Preaching with minimal reliance on a manuscript is a learned skill, not inborn. With effort anyone can do it.

(2) There is no one way of achieving it. You have to learn what works for you. It does take time and effort, but it may be the best time you've ever spent.

The obvious solution to avoid reading sermons is the worst solution: Not write the sermon out at all. There are occasions when we may not have time to write a sermon out in full, but those should be rare. For long-term growth and improvement in preaching there is no substitute for careful preparation of a manuscript. Pastors who skimp on writing inevitably skimp on preparation, and despite whatever native ability they may have, they soon become shallow and trite in the pulpit.

The challenge is to prepare the sermon well, then deliver it well.

A young pastor I knew was basically a reader, until the congregation added a contemporary worship service. With the informality of the service, the pastors decided not to use a pulpit at all. Panicked at the prospect of having nothing in front of him, the younger pastor first used a music stand, but that was too awkward and flimsy. Finally he decided to take the plunge and stand before the congregation with nothing in front of him. "I was scared to death," he told me later, "and the first sermons were awful. But now I'm getting used to it, and I have to admit I'm a better preacher now."

More informative was the comment of a layperson in the congregation, who told me about the new preaching style at the services. "The youth pastor is really good at it," she said. "He used to read his sermons, and I thought he was abstract and boring. But now he talks straight at us, and he's really good."

The pastor thinks his sermons aren't very well organized, because sometimes, as he says, he "has to rearrange things as I go along." But the listener says, "I know what he's saying now."

My suggestion is that every pastor should preach at least occasionally with no notes at all. It's not easy, but you will become a much better communicator!

Piecemeal

How does one learn to speak without a manuscript? One way is to start with short talks. All pastors are called upon for shorter meditations — Sunday school, devotions at church groups. Do them without notes, which is not nearly so daunting as a Sunday sermon.

Once you are comfortable speaking for two, three or four minutes without notes, select parts of the sermon to deliver without looking at notes. Don't even take those notes into the pulpit.

The easiest parts of the sermon to deliver without notes are stories and illustrations, because telling a story without notes seems natural.

The next step is to do the opening and closing without notes, because they are the most crucial times in the sermon to speak directly to the congregation.

Learning The Manuscript

How does one learn a manuscript? Try different methods and decide what works for you. Here are some tips I've learned from pastors:

(1) Some people are good at memorizing, even getting up early Sunday morning and learning the sermon before the service. Most of us are not proficient at memorizing, but there are other ways of learning the sermon.

(2) What works best for me is to read out loud several times, looking at the manuscript less and less. I usually take the manuscript into the pulpit.

(3) Mark your manuscript with underlining or yellow marker. The important words will stand out when you look down.

(4) Write down key words in a wide left margin. You can glance at those words without looking at the text itself.

(5) Some pastors follow the Peter Marshall format of writing. Each paragraph begins at the left, with following sentences indented. Important phrases or parallel thoughts are indented even further and written one under the other. Each new section of the sermon begins on the left, easily spotted in a short glance.

(6) Some pastors find it helpful actually to practice in the pulpit.

Whatever works to free yourself from the manuscript, do it. There is no one way for everybody. The less you read, the better preacher you'll be.

Use Of Voice

"Change grabs attention" is a rule which applies not only to different types of sermons, but also to the use of your voice.

My high school voice teacher used to repeat to us, "Be smooth, be smooth, be smoo-oo-ooth!" It was good advice for nervous school children whose problem was being so tongue-tied we could hardly put three sentences together without stuttering, stammering and stumbling all over our words. But that advice is deadly to a preacher, because too smooth is boring.

I had a college teacher with a marvelous voice — deep, resonant, and smooth. At some point during almost every lecture that semester I fell asleep, and I received my worst college grade in that course. That wonderful voice lulled me to sleep. It was so-o-o smooth, with no change in pitch, volume or speed.

A smooth, even speaking tone becomes monotonous, and people's attention drifts away. As soon as you change anything, people are back with you. The simplest thing to change is volume. Pulpit thumping and shouting gets attention because it's a change. However, preachers who bellow all the time soon become as monotonous as one who drones at a moderate level.

My former seminary teacher George Aus was extremely effective at the other end of the sound spectrum. He would be speaking along with his strident Brooklyn-bred tone, but when he wanted to make a point, he would pause, lean over the lectern, and drop his voice to a whisper. Anybody who had been looking out the window until then immediately leaned to the edge of his seat to catch what he was saying. One could hear a pin drop in the classroom.

It was effective because it was a change.

Changing speed is equally effective. Most of us speak too fast. Being nervous causes that. On the other hand some people speak so slowly and evenly that they lack energy. The key to keeping the audience's attention is to alter your pace. When you come to a key sentence, pause, then speak it slowly and with emphasis. People will listen, sensing it is an important statement because you said it differently. Conversely, if you're speaking evenly, speed up when you make a point, and people will listen because they sense the increased energy and intensity.

Every now and then a preacher gets a sentence garbled up and stumbles around trying to get back on track. Or one simply gets lost. One usually has to stop, get one's bearings and have another run at it. Such a break can be extremely embarrassing for a speaker, but it probably helps the sermon more than harms it, because as soon as the preacher starts to stumble, even those who are counting bricks on the wall or filling in the es and os in the bulletin snap back to attention. Something is different, and they listen.

Carpentry Work On The Pulpit — "Up And Out"

In trying to increase your eye contact with the congregation, one of your chief problems may be the pulpit itself. It's probably built wrong.

"Never preach with your sermon three inches from your belt buckle," a teacher once told me. Pulpits are often constructed for people barely over five feet tall, with the manuscript two feet below us. No wonder we preach looking like one of those toy ducks bobbing up and down in front of a water glass!

Get your sermon notes "up and out," up higher and away from you, so you don't have to look straight down to see your notes. The pulpit in my last parish was the best I've ever preached from. The actual lectern was low and unusable, but somebody had fashioned two one-by-six boards in an upside-down "L" shape covering the front and top of the fluorescent bulb along the front of the pulpit. I cut my sermons in half, 8 1/2- by-5 1/2-inches and laid them on the top board. I could look straight at the audience and glance down at the sermon without moving my head.

Recently I preached in a church with the worst pulpit I've ever used. The gorgeous carved wood pulpit was a nightmare for a preacher. The top was about as big as a *Time* magazine cover, with no shelves, no place for a Bible, other sheets of paper, or even a wristwatch. Worse yet, it was built for a pastor about four-foot ten-inches tall. I would have preferred to stand somewhere else, but the microphone was mounted right on the pulpit.

Many pastors build a simple wooden platform to set on top of the pulpit, raising the manuscript. A simple adjustment to pulpit architecture may be of great help!

"Non-Verbal" Communication

Like it or not, how you look in the pulpit must be consistent with the message you're speaking. This doesn't mean that you need to have all your teeth capped and a hairdresser in the sacristy before each service. Far from it. This involves more than just physical appearance.

We know that non-verbal factors are part of communication. We will not be convincing when we speak of the joy of the gospel if we look as if we have a stomach ache. You won't persuade anybody by speaking of the love we have for each other if you preach in such grim tones one would think you're angry at your listeners. If you speak without energy or enthusiasm, your message will come across as lethargic as your delivery.

Any good public speaker is nervous. Tension makes us alert and adds energy to speaking. However, nerves can also freeze our personality and give a wooden quality to our appearance. "Bring your personality into the pulpit with you," I say regularly to beginning preachers. Ideally one should be nervous enough to be on edge, but relaxed enough to appear natural in the pulpit.

Our own commitment to the gospel proclamation is part of the "non-verbal" message we send. Listening to sermons Sunday after Sunday, listeners soon sense the pastor's urgency about the gospel. One of the saddest comments I ever heard followed a sermon of a pastor soon to retire. We were close friends, and I knew that he was exhausted from his parish work and could hardly wait to retire. After the sermon a wise and perceptive woman said to me, "He really doesn't believe what he's saying, does he?" He did believe it, but his whole tone and demeanor was that he was tired of preaching. The non-verbal message overshadowed the words themselves.

Tape Yourself

Actors and television performers always work with cameras, because they know that what counts is what the audience sees and hears, not what they think they look like. We preachers usually enter the pulpit with no idea how we actually come across.

Speakers have an image of how they sound and look, and it's usually wrong. Every one of us has the experience of listening to ourselves on audio tape and thinking, "That doesn't sound like my voice at all!" You're right. What you hear booming around in your own sinus cavity sounds rich and full to you, but it is not your speaking voice. What you hear on tape is what your listeners hear.

Voice quality can be improved, as anybody who has taken voice training knows. Voice teachers work with students to lower the tone of one's voice, relax and open up the throat passage.

Listening to yourself on tape enables you to hear yourself as others hear you. In my own case, I noticed that my diction was not clear — gonna, whatcha. Such phrases are normal in conversation, but they make public speech slurry and indistinct.

Scottish poet Robert Burns could have been thinking of the preachers he listened to when he wrote almost two centuries ago:

> *O wad some Power the giftie give us*
> *To see oursels as ithers see us!*
> *It wad frae mony a blunder free us ...*
> (From "To a Louse")

Today we have the gift to "see oursels as ithers see us." Videotape yourself. Your audience not only hears you, it sees you, and with a video you can see yourself as it sees you. If you don't have a camcorder, somebody in the congregation does, and with modern zoom lenses, the camera can stand inconspicuously in the back. For the best quality of sound, plug the microphone into the church public address system. If that

102

isn't possible, the microphone on the camera will be too far away for good sound, but it will be sufficient for you. Watching yourself will be the most depressing but the most profitable few minutes of your whole week.

For example, for the first five years in my ministry, my wife constantly told me, "Why do you look so mad in the pulpit?" I never believed her, because I did not feel angry. Not until I saw myself on video was I appalled to realize how right she had been. I looked angry because I was tense and nervous.

Honest Delivery

Much is said about "charisma," that extra touch a great communicator has. Charisma isn't the issue for pastors. Charistmatic speakers draw attention to themselves. Our concern is that the message be heard. For that to happen, good delivery is essential.

Some think effective public speaking is a matter of bombast — shouting, florid gestures and entertaining jokes. Nothing is further from the truth. You don't have to become somebody else or imitate other speakers to be a better preacher. You might make a powerful first impression if you do that, but in the long run you will lose credibility, because a congregation who knows you on the weekdays will soon figure out that you're not the same person in the pulpit.

The secret to truly effective speaking is being yourself in the pulpit. Deliver that sermon as well as you can, Sunday after Sunday, and you will be a faithful servant of the gospel!

Preaching And Pastoral Ministry

A word must be added about the connection between preaching and pastoral ministry. With the competition of television the expectations for effective preaching is higher than in the past. Yet the pastor has one huge advantage over television performers: The people who listen on Sunday also know the pastor as one who teaches, visits in homes, hospitals and nursing homes, counsels, baptizes, marries, buries — deeply involved in the lives of the people.

In the long run effective preaching is more than the techniques of good vocabulary, structure, delivery, and so on — as important as they are. Good preaching is part of the larger fabric of the ministry we do the rest of the week.

The Episcopal church ran a series of ads a few years ago to highlight the importance of local congregations. I remember seeing one on a poster in an airport. It pictured a chalice and paten on top of a television set with a pastor's stole draped over it. The caption read, "How often does your TV set give you communion?"

When you stand in the pulpit, your people see somebody who has visited them at the sickbed, talked with them in the grocery store, buried their grandmother, baptized their babies, taken their children to Bible camp, drunk coffee in the parish hall and so on. You preach on Sunday morning with your whole ministry behind you — something that the most spectacular preacher or performer on television can never match.

This became very clear to me some years ago when I was part of a church but not the pastor. My first impression was that the preacher was not very good. The content was not imaginative, the delivery was not stimulating, and the voice was barely audible. Then I got to know the pastor, his affection for children and the elderly, his faithfulness at visiting hospitals and nursing homes. During those months I concluded he was a much better preacher than I had thought at first.

Of course he had not changed his preaching at all in that time. My perception had changed because I came to know him as a pastor, and he was a splendid pastor. He became a better preacher in my eyes because I saw him in a new way. In retrospect I would say he should have worked more diligently on his preaching, but I also realized how preaching is tied to a pastor's total ministry.

Verbum Dei Manet In Aeternum

"The Word of God remains forever." The last word about preaching in a new age of communication is that the measure of true preaching remains the same: the faithful proclamation of God's Word. We return to the truth stated at the start of this book from Luther's 95 Theses: "The true treasure of the church is the most holy gospel of the glory and grace of God."

The final measure of preaching is fidelity to the Word. Communication styles will continue to change, and we shall continue to adapt, but the gospel of Jesus remains constant.

It is precisely the love for this Word which compels us to understand the nature of today's communication and to use all the skill we can to convey the great and wonderful message entrusted to us.

Helmut Thielicke described his despair at sermons where the "once relevant proclamation has been swathed with cotton." In the midst of the chapter he suddenly breaks the flow of his thought:

I interrupt here for a moment, for I have just returned from hearing a sermon which by its breath-taking banality has thrown me completely off the track. So many words and nothing said! . . . Empty straw, all the cliches that just seemed to flood into the preacher's head! And knowing that it was all pious blather . . . he turned on the rhetorical explosions in order to dispel the boredom by pseudo-dramatizations . . . And all the while it was such inflated nothingness that was the more painful simply because . . . he obviously had not worked on it at all or perhaps for only a short half hour. I could not help but think of the precision with which even a little juggler on the stage of a provincial variety theater operates, the honest and disciplined work he does, and the offense that would be taken if he showed the slightest sign of sloppiness. Apparently it is possible to handle the Word of God sloppily, but obviously you can't do the same thing with juggling balls. How shocking is the display of slovenliness in this of all places![57]

105

The words of a parishioner constantly come back to me as I prepare a sermon: "It's a tough world out there, pastor. I need to hear the gospel when I come to church. I really need it!"

Many such people listen to you every Sunday. They need the Word of Life. We dare not let them down!

Endnotes

Foreword

1. *Luther's Works,* Philadelphia: Muhlenberg Press, 1957, Vol. 31, 31.

Chapter 1

2. James Monaco, "The TV Plexus," *Sight and Sound* magazine, Winter 78/79, Vol. 48. Quoted in *Television and American Culture: The Reference Shelf,* Vol. 53, No. 2, ed. Carl Lowe, New York: The H.W. Wilson Company, 1981, 14.

3. John Killinger, *The 11 O'Clock News and Other Experimental Sermons,* Nashville: Abingdon Press, 1975, 11.

4. Richard A. Jensen, *Thinking In Story: Preaching In A Post-literate Age,* Lima, Ohio: The CSS Publishing Company, 1993. This book argues that this "shift from one communication era to another . . . calls upon us to seriously re-think most of what we do." (p. 8) Jensen believes that we have moved from a "literate culture," which is dominated by print and thinks in ideas, to an "oral-aural culture," where people hear and see through electronic media.

5. For a broader view on the relationship of television with religion or the church, see William F. Fore's *Television and Religion. The Shaping of Faith, Values and Culture,* Minneapolis: Augsburg Publishing House, 1987. The thesis of this book is that television is usurping a role which until recently has been the role of the church in our society, namely, to

shape our system of values, embody our faith, and express our cultural center. This shift, from a religious center to what I call a technological center, is ominous ... [Television is] "an alternative religion which is wooing people into a whole new way of thinking about, and living in, our world" (11, 24, 130). See also Gregor T. Goethals, *The TV Ritual: Worship at the Video Altar*, Boston: Beacon Press book, 1981; Kate Moody, *Growing up on Television: The TV Effect*, New York: Times Books, 1980; Frank Mankiewicz and Joel Swerdlow, *Remote Control: Television and the Manipulation of American Life*, New York: New York Times Book Company, Inc., 1978.

6. Roy P. Madsen, *The Impact of Film: How Ideas are Communicated through Cinema and Television*, New York: Macmillan Publishing Co., Inc., 1973, 27.

7. Peter Conrad, *Television — the Medium and its Manners*, Boston, London, Henley: Routledge & Kegan Paul, 1982, 46, 48.

8. Neil Postman argues pessimistically that television as an entertainment medium "has made entertainment itself the natural format for the representation of all experience ... Thinking does not play well on television." *Amusing Ourselves to Death: Public Discourse in the Age of Show Business*, New York: Viking Press, 1985, 87f. See also Jacques Ellul, *The Humiliation of the Word*, Grand Rapids: Eerdmans, 1985.

9. Ellen Goodman, Minneapolis *Star Tribune*, January 1991, 12A.

10. Jensen, op. cit., 45, 46.

Chapter 2

11. Jerry L. Schmalenberger, homiletics teacher and president of Pacific Lutheran Theological Seminary, Berkeley, California. "Three Shots for Lutherans," *Lutheran Partners,* July/August, 1992, 23.

12. Patricia Wilson-Kastner, *Imagery for Preaching,* Minneapolis: Fortress Press, 1989, 19.

13. Kate Moody, *Growing Up on Television,* New York: Times Books, 1980, 37.

14. Donald Macleod, *The Problem of Preaching,* Philadelphia: Fortress, 1987, 79.

Chapter 3

15. Elizabeth Achtemeier, *Creative Preaching,* Nashville: Abingdon Press, 1980, 14.

16. Schmalenberger, op. cit., 23.

17. Fred B. Craddock, *As One Without Authority,* Nashville: Abingdon Press, 1960, 60.

18. William Shakespeare, *Macbeth*, Act V, Scene 5.

19. Walter Brueggemann, *Finally Comes the Poet: Daring Speech for Proclamation,* Minneapolis: Fortress, 1989, 1, 3. This book is very helpful for preachers, not only because it urges a new, poetic kind of speech, but also because it offers themes for preaching to this modern world, particularly using the rich resources of the Old Testament.

20. Jensen, op. cit., 10. "... I have moved from advice for 'telling the story' as a way of preaching to advocating story

109

as a way of thought: 'thinking in story.' ... I am seriously proposing a kind of paradigm shift for preachers shaped by the literate world's approach to preaching ... We have learned to think in ideas. We have learned to preach sermons that were primarily filled with ideas. Now we must also learn how to think in stories."

21. For example, one of Princeton University historian James M. McPherson's chapters in *Abraham Lincoln and the Second American Revolution* is titled "How Lincoln Won the War with Metaphors." His thesis is that Lincoln's speeches were effective in large part because he knew how to illustrate and persuade with metaphors and examples easily understood by his listeners. (New York: Oxford University Press, 1990, 93f.)

22. William Bausch, *Storytelling — Imagination and Faith,* Mystic, Connecticut: Twenty-Third Publication, 1984, 11.

23. Brueggeman, op. cit., 11.

24. Helmut Thielicke, "The Meaning of Prayer," in *20 Centuries of Great Preaching,* Volume 12, Waco, Texas: Word, Inc., 1971, 233.

25. Frederick Buechner, "The Hungering Dark," in *The Twentieth Century Pulpit,* ed. James W. Cox, Nashville: Abingdon Press, 1978, 27.

26. Brueggemann, op. cit., 11.

27. Robert Hughes, "The Controlling Image: One Key to Sermon Unity," *Academy Accents* (newsletter of the Academy of Preachers), Winter 1991, 2.

28. Wilson-Kastner, op. cit., 49.

29. Michael Rogness, *Augsburg Sermons: Series A. Gospels,* Minneapolis: Augsburg Publishing House, 1974, 173f.

30. Jensen. op. cit., 144.

Chapter 4

31. Cited by Helmut Thielicke, *Encounter with Spurgeon,* Philadelphia: Fortress, 1963, 193.

32. Donald Macleod, op. cit., 47.

33. H. Grady Davis, *Design for Preaching,* Philadelphia: Muhlenberg Press, 1958, 43. Cf. his helpful chapter on "The Text as Source," where he outlines the movement from text to the "sermon idea," 41-57.

34. Charles H. Spurgeon, "A New Year's Benediction," in *This Great Company: A Treasury of Great Sermons by Outstanding Preachers of the Christian Tradition,* ed. David Poling, New Canaan, Connecticut: Keats Publishing, Inc., 1976, 45f.

35. James Stewart, "Why Go To Church?" in *The Twentieth Century Pulpit,* ed. James W. Cox, Nashville: Abingdon Press, 1978, 226-236.

36. Alvin N. Rogness, *Who Shall Be God?,* Minneapolis: Augsburg Publishing House, 1954, 67f.

Chapter 5

37. Charles L. Bartow, *The Preaching Moment: A Guide to Sermon Delivery,* Nashville: Abingdon Press, 1980, 21.

38. David Buttrick, *Homiletic Moves and Structures,* Philadelphia: Fortress Press, 1987, 305, 316. For an extended and helpful discussion about various methods of structuring the sermon, see his chapters 18-25, 285f.

39. Eugene Lowry, *The Homiletical Plot,* Atlanta: John Knox Press, 1980, 21.

40. Ibid., 21.

41. Bartow, op. cit., 22. He is quoting Charlotte I. Lee, *Oral Interpretation,* New York: Houghton Mifflin Co., 1971, 27-28.

42. Lowry, op. cit., 15.

43. Ibid., 25. He adds that his students have found it helpful to remember these steps with the following abbreviations: 1) Oops, 2) Ugh, 3) Aha, 4) Whee, and 5) Yeah!

44. Peter Marshall, "Under Sealed Orders," in *20 Centuries of Great Preaching,* Vol. 12, eds. Clyde E. Fant, Jr., and William M. Pinson, Waco: Word Books, Publisher, 1971, 31.

45. Ibid., 42

46. Martin Luther King, Jr., *The Twentieth Century Pulpit,* Vol. I, ed. James W. Cox, Nashville: Abingdon Press, 1978, 115f.

47. Ibid., 121.

48. Ibid.

49. Ibid., 123.

50. *The Twentieth Century Pulpit,* Vol. II, ed. James W. Cox, Nashville: Abingdon Press, 1981, 47f.

Chapter 6

51. Killinger, op. cit., 22.

52. See Edward Markquart's *Quest for Better Preaching,* Chapter 12, "The Importance of Variety of Forms," Minneapolis: Augsburg Publishing House, 1985, 203f.

53. Peter Marshall, "Were You There?", sermon on audio cassette in the library of Bethel Theological Seminary, St. Paul, Minnesota.

54. Ralph Stone, *Circus, Parable, Construction,* St. Louis: The Bethany Press, 1961, 87.

55. Jensen, op. Cit., 57.

Chapter 7

56. Homer K. Buerlein, *How To Preach More Powerful Sermons,* Philadelphia: The Westminster Press, 1986, 14.

57. Helmut Thielicke, "The Breakdown of Words and Their Revival," in *The Trouble with the Church,* New York: Harper & Row, Publishers, 1965, 48, 43.